The Single Mom's Little Guide to Building a Big Life

By:
Summerlin Conner

Also by *Summerlin Conner:*

The Three of Us: A Brutally Honest, Often Hilarious, and Sometimes Heartbreaking Memoir of One Mom's Adventures in Single Parenting

For all the single moms out there,
the strongest women on Earth

Table of Contents

Chapter 1: *Single mommas*

Chapter 2: *Who do you want to be?*

Chapter 3: *Getting your mind right*

Chapter 4: *Feeling good*

Chapter 5: *Relationships*

Chapter 6: *Bringing home the bacon*

Chapter 7: *The three of us*

Chapter 8: *Wishing and hoping*

*Following chapter 8 is a list of resources that I have found helpful over the years.

Chapter 1:
Single mommas

Before we even get started, let me just go ahead and throw this out there: when I became a single mom, I was a HOT

MESS. I mean like level-ten hot mess. Like embarrassing hot mess. Rock bottom hot mess. I will elaborate more later, but, for now, just know that this disastrous time period involved gaining thirty pounds, loads of anger and anxiety, foreclosure on my house, shame-worthy jealousy, depression, hopelessness, and much more. Yikes.

So, without question, I have been to the depths of rock bottom and I know how to turn things around. I was able to, mostly kicking and screaming, get my life back on track and get to living again. I was able to pull myself out of the mud and dust myself off and start over. And believe me when I say that there was a lot of mud.

Are you currently in the mud? Are you up to your neck in thick, stinky mud? Or maybe you just have a little dirt on your knees? Or perhaps you are somewhere in the middle? Regardless, if you are in any way, shape, or form looking to build a better life, then you came to the right place.

More than anything, I want that for you. I want you to reclaim your life and make your comeback. I want you to build a life that you love and a life that makes you excited to get out of bed in the morning. I want you to learn to love your life (or at least think it's pretty darn good).

Who were you before you became a single mom? Or, more importantly, who were you when you were at your best? What did your life look like when you felt good, had confidence, and had (most of) your ducks in a row?

Or maybe you have NEVER completely been the awesome person you have always wanted to be. Maybe you have always held a vision in your mind of what your most badass self would look and act like, but you feel like you never really got there. Well, can you picture her now?

Take one minute now and picture what your perfect life would look like. What would you and your kids be doing? What kind of job (or no job!) would you be doing? How would you feel? What would your financial situation look like? What would your social life look like? How does your body look and feel? What would you do in any spare time that you have? What would your dreams and goals be?

Here's how I envision my coolest, most awesome self: First of all, I look awesome. I look healthy, in shape, and sun-kissed 365 days of the year. I eat healthy food mostly but also splurge when I want to. I feel good. Like, deep down in my bones, I feel good. I am always smiling because I am just downright happy, and I feel blessed. I have a great job that I really like. I make enough money to feel comfortable and I don't feel constantly stressed about money or like I am always living paycheck to paycheck. I sometimes do things with friends. I go on dates if I want to, and I don't go on dates if I don't want to. Regardless, I DEFINITELY don't give my time to anyone who doesn't treat me like gold. Maybe a handsome, funny, and kind Prince Charming comes along and we fall madly in love and get married. And he treats my kids and me like we are the best thing that's ever happened to him. Or maybe he never comes along and I live happily ever after by myself. When my kids are with their dad, I relax and use the time to do whatever the heck I want that makes me feel good. I feel confident in myself, and I am no longer weighed down by guilt or shame or the past. I don't feel constantly exhausted, depressed, and anxious. I don't wake up in the morning and dread the day ahead.

I have a stable, amicable relationship with my kids' dad and there are no more fights, hard feelings, drama or emotional strings. Just harmony. And I have a peaceful, amicable relationship with my kids' stepmom. And last, but above all else, I have an incredible, loving, wouldn't-have-it-any-other-way relationship with my two kids. We communicate with one another, laugh together, and they both lean on me and trust me. We take fun vacations together. They feel so comfortable with me that they love to talk about their hopes and dreams. I feel so incredibly blessed. I just all-around feel happy with my life. I am free!

I could keep going and going and I could also get a lot more detailed, but that's the gist of it. That's how I envision my life when I think of the best, most free me. That's the vision I hold in my head when someone asks me what my goals are.

So, where are you right now in your single mom journey? Are you just getting started in this adventure? Are you in the trenches of your rock bottom? Are you digging yourself out of the mud? Are you already rocking your most extraordinary life?

Look, we all know being a single mom is HARD. I mean really freaking hard. There are always going to be some things we can't change. We can't change the long hours that come with this single mom job. We can't change the occasional and inevitable tantrums that our kids will throw and we will have to deal with all alone. We can't change the fact that we are single moms. Well, I mean we could get remarried and technically not be a single mom anymore, but that's a different story. My point is there will be lots of (sometimes not so great) things that we are stuck dealing with as single moms. But we can always work on ourselves and we can always find ways to feel some joy. We can keep going. We can always try to build a better life for ourselves and our babies even when it feels like we can't go on one more freaking minute.

Just because we are single moms doesn't mean that we have to be doomed to a life of misery or exhaustion (well, sometimes maybe exhaustion) or shame or despair. Even though it doesn't always feel like it, we deserve to be happy and live a full life. And our kids deserve a momma who is happy.

I, for one, have consistently been guilty of putting my kids and their needs WAY ahead of mine. And I wouldn't change a thing I have done, and I will always be happy to put my kids first. BUT…sometimes it's too easy to get lost in putting your kids first. Sometimes we get so focused on our kids' needs and their health and happiness that we severely damage our own health and happiness.

When I first got divorced, I was so crazy concerned about my kids and so crazy consumed with how they were handling the situation. I was filled with guilt about getting divorced because I was sure it would ruin my kids' lives. So what did I do to make up for that? I threw ALL of my needs out the window and only focused on the two of them. I quit exercising because I felt bad for leaving them in the gym daycare. I stopped socializing entirely because that would have meant I would be spending money on something besides them and possibly leaving them with a babysitter. I went broke spending money on them to give them things I thought would make them happy. I altogether quit taking care of myself. And you know what happened? I went broke, got severely depressed and anxious, and gained thirty pounds. Yikes.

Let me quickly give you a snapshot of a day in the life of me about five years ago:

A Typical Day (circa 2015)

5:30am: My alarm goes off and I already want to cry because I already dread living another day in this existence. I am already exhausted because I most likely tossed and turned all night due to my mind racing about bills piling up and how on Earth will I get the kids to all of their activities and, holy hell, how much I hate myself for eating those cookies.

7:00am: Get the kids up and off to school. I try to be as upbeat, positive, and encouraging as I can. Meanwhile, really wishing I could drop the kids at school and go straight back home, get back in bed, and sleep the day away.

8:00am: Head out to my job that I absolutely hate. My boss drives me crazy, and the work itself is exhausting and unfulfilling. I feel stressed all day long and like I am going to crack at any minute.

9:00am: I get a text from a friend inviting me to a big holiday party that is coming up. There will be lots of couples and a gift exchange and I will need to buy a new dress to wear since I no longer fit into my current dresses. Um, how fast can I come up with an excuse? This is a definite no thanks for me.

10:00am: Oh my gosh, I am going to lose my crap if I get one more call from the mortgage company. I can't even deal with that right now.

12:00pm: I take a quick lunch break. How do I spend my time while I am eating? Probably stalking the Facebook of my ex-husband's new girlfriend. Or maybe rehashing that snarky text I got from my ex-husband. Anything that would most likely get my blood boiling or the tears flowing.

1:00pm: Ugh, I have to go to Target. Usually, I love browsing at Target. But not these days. Going to Target means you are, most likely, going to see someone you know. And, these days, I don't want to see ANYONE that I know. Why? Because I am embarrassed by how

I look. I am embarrassed by my life situation. And I am not even slightly in the mood for small talk. Especially with someone who seems like they have their life together. Which pretty much feels like everyone but me. So, instead of going to the Target right down the road from my house, I drive twenty-five minutes away to the Target in the next town over. In this Target, I can breathe. I can relax. I can be anonymous.

3:00pm: Time to pick up the kids from school. By this point I am completely exhausted and would give anything for a nap and a two-week vacation in Tahiti. Instead, I try to pull myself together. I get the kids a snack and head home. That is, if I have enough money in my bank account to get them a snack. When we get home, there are a million choices for what I can do. Help the kids with homework. Cut the grass that seems ten feet high. Work on my resume so I can find a better job. Mop the floors that probably haven't been mopped in months. Address the giant stack of bills on the kitchen counter. Clean the bathroom. And on and on and on. It really doesn't matter what I choose to do because, no matter what, I will still most likely feel guilty and beat myself up for not getting ENOUGH done. I mean, why can't I be a better mom? Why can't I have it all together like the other moms? Why can't I get it all done like every other mom seems to? Something is obviously very wrong with me, and I suck at life, and I seriously ought to be so freaking ashamed of myself. I just want to cry.

4:00pm: I go to start the dishwasher and it won't start. Are you serious? So the freaking dishwasher is broken. Well, I guess I will be hand washing all of the dishes from now on because I certainly do not have the money to get that fixed. My choices are that I can either get the dishwasher fixed or buy the kids Christmas presents. Well, I better go by some new dish gloves because the kids are getting Christmas presents.

4:30pm: I just got a text from one of my friends telling me that she heard my ex-husband is in Paris with his girlfriend right now and that he bought a new sports car last week. I can't even.

5:00pm: Make the kids dinner. I really want to get some exercise or breathe some fresh air but I am so overwhelmed with life that I don't even know how to go about making that happen. So I stick with making dinner. I had hoped to make myself this yummy looking vegan recipe I saw on Pinterest but I am just too damn tired. So I cook the kids spaghetti and I eat that with them.

7:00pm: By this time, I have a headache and I can barely keep my eyes open. But I get the kids bathed and ready for bed. Here comes the only moment of the day when I will feel genuine joy, love, and happiness. When I tuck my kids into bed and we hug and tell each other how much we love one another. Those five minutes of love and snuggles and sweetness make the world okay for just a brief moment. And then it's over. My kids sometimes still sleep in bed with me. I know that may not be the best situation but I am way too tired to try to change things. Instead, I just beat myself up for being a horrible mom because I am not doing everything perfectly.

8:00pm: Finally, the kids are asleep and I have a minute of quiet. I guess I will spend a few minutes stalking my ex-husband's girlfriend's Pinterest boards. Wait, did I just hear something outside? Holy crap, what if an ax murderer trying to break in? What if they get in and try to kill the kids and me? I am utterly alone in handling this. I am the only adult here and I have to be brave and fight off this ax murderer all by myself.

9:00pm: Okay, it was not an ax murderer. Just a raccoon. Thank God. And, while I am at it, can you hear me, God? I seriously need help with my life. I am weary. I am exhausted. I am lonely. I am tired. I feel defeated.

9:15pm: I just can't do it. I don't have the energy to even try not to eat a million cookies. So I eat a million cookies. And I feel comforted. For just a minute. And then I hate myself.

9:30pm: I go to sleep already dreading doing it all over again tomorrow.

If this sounds even remotely familiar to you, all I can say is, I get it. I 100% get it. And this is just a snapshot of a typical day in my life back then. There were days when it was five hundred times worse than this. There were days when I would lose my shit and send a horrible text to my ex. There were days when I would get a call from the mortgage company wanting $17,000 by Friday. There were days when I would sob myself to sleep.

The only thing that was consistent in my life back then was my love for my kids. I would do anything for them. They were the ones that kept me going. They were the light of my life.

I am convinced that we single mommas sometimes get so lost in loving our little ones that we forget the importance of taking care of ourselves too. I think we sometimes believe that, just because we are single moms, we somehow don't deserve a full life. Sometimes we feel like, since we got divorced (or split up or whatever), we owe our kids our lives. I am 100% guilty of feeling this way. I have definitely felt, numerous times, like, since I put my kids through this, I owe them the rest of my life and happiness. Wow, that's a big freaking heap of guilt and sacrifice.

So here's where we have a problem. I could talk all day about how to build a better life and how you can live the life of your dreams. I could tell you twenty billion different ways to start making positive changes. But here's the thing. None of that matters. It doesn't matter how good of an argument I have for making positive improvements. Why? Because if you don't believe you deserve the best life or you don't believe that your kids will benefit from these things, then you, as a single momma, are not going to be open to making these changes. Most likely, you are going to make excuses for why you don't deserve a beautiful life or why you think it would be selfish of you to live your best life. As single moms, it's really freaking hard to even consider our needs without also considering our babies' needs.

I want to stop here and just point that out again. Being the amazing human beings that they are, single moms require a completely different approach to self-improvement than anyone else. Why? Because I would argue that there are no other humans on this earth who ALWAYS think of their kids first when making every single decision. Who always make their kids' needs their top priority. Who always sacrifice their wants and needs for the sake of their children. Who would step out in front of a bus to save their kids.

I know all moms love their kids. Of course they do! But I just feel, on a really deep level, like there is something extra, extra special about single moms and the love and feelings they have for their kids. It's like an enhanced form of love and protection and dedication. To me, it's an extra special bond that I am not entirely positive would be there if their dad and I had stayed together. I really don't know. But what I do know is that I love them more than anything in this world and, like I've said before, if you mess with them, I will cut you. Just kidding. Maybe. ;)

So, how do we build a full, happy, healthy life when we feel this way? Well, as backwards as it sounds, we have to start by thinking of our kids. What?!? I thought this book was about building MY best life?!? I know, I know; just hear me out…

Sometimes, when I am lost in thought, it occurs to me to look at my life from my daughter's vantage point. What does she see? What kind of life am I modeling for her? What kind of life do I want for her?

Or my son? What kind of woman am I modeling for him? What kind of woman would I want for him in his future relationships?

And when I am an old lady and on my little deathbed, what do I want my kids to remember me for?

And this is when my eyes really open up. This is the exact moment that it all becomes crystal clear. If a life lived in stress, unhappiness, and shame would not be okay for my kids, then why on Earth would it be okay for me? If a life lived overworked, exhausted, overweight, self-sacrificed, and lonely would not be okay for my babies, then, in what world is that okay for me??

Because I am, after all, their number one role model for what life as a woman looks like. I am their definition of what a single mom is. How I live my life defines to them what a single mom's life looks like. That's HUGE.

When I really think hard about this, it makes everything so clear to me. All of the times when I thought I was "doing the right thing" by completely sacrificing my well-being and sanity for my kids, I now realize that may not have been the best way to go. Ouch.

What do I want my kids to see when they look at me? What do I want them to learn from my behavior? Who do I want to be in their eyes? Do I want to be a woman who is completely run-down, depressed, unhappy, and has no life of her own? Do I want to be a woman who is constantly angry with her ex-husband and constantly dissing his new wife? Or do I want to be a woman who is happy, engaged in life, and working towards my dreams?

When my daughter looks at me, what do I want her to see? A tired, grumpy, unhealthy woman who is struggling and barely surviving? A woman who has no hopes and dreams? A woman who takes care of her kids, eats, works, and sleeps and nothing else? A woman who doesn't take consistent care of her body? A woman with no boundaries or self-respect? A woman who lets men treat her like crap? A bitter woman who can't let go of the past?

Or do I want her to see a vibrant, happy woman who is working towards her hopes and dreams? A woman who takes care of her body and mind? A woman who has self-respect, boundaries, and loves herself? A woman who acknowledges the tough times she has been through but still sees an even brighter future? A single mom who adores her two kids and feels like her heart and life is so full that she could just burst?

And what about my son? What kind of woman do I want to model for him? How do I want him to see women? After all, this will most likely affect who he chooses to marry and how he will, one day, treat his wife. Do I want him to see a broken woman with no life left in her? Do I want him to see a helpless woman who has given up? Do I want him to see a woman with no boundaries and no love for herself? Do I want him to have to feel responsible for her feelings and her needs?

Or do I want him to see a woman who is filled with self-love and self-respect? Do I want him to see a woman who can not only take care of herself, but do it happily? Do I want him to see a healthy, vibrant woman who is filled with joy?

What do you think? What would you like your kids to see?

Here's another way to put it that always hits me right in the chest and takes my breath away. Did you know that kids often feel stressed and responsible when we are unhappy? Wait, what? Yes. On a deep level, children will often feel our unhappiness, our unfulfillment, and our general vibe. And they will, in turn, feel stressed about that and possibly even responsible. Ugh. How awfully sad is that? Knowing this, it would appear as though all the self-sacrificing and ignoring of my own needs to serve my kids could potentially backfire.

Here's one example. Imagine that it's a Saturday afternoon and you really want (and need) to go to the gym and exercise because it's been forever and you're really out of shape and it makes you feel so good. And it's really freaking good for your mental health and sanity. It's only one hour. But your kids HATE the gym daycare. They cry and throw a horrendous tantrum if you even suggest going there. So, what do you do? In the past, nine times out of ten I would have skipped the gym because my kids didn't want to go. And then (and this is SO embarrassing) I would most likely spend the afternoon pouting and cranky because I didn't "get" to go. And to be completely honest, I would probably make myself feel better by eating cookies. Ugh. And you know who will pick up on those vibes of misery and negativity? Yep. The kids. They will soak it right up and feel it right along with you, even if neither you nor they realize it.

But what if we played this scenario out a different way? What if I had not given in to my kids' tantrum and instead gone ahead and gone to the gym? What if I would have made my needs important too? Let's be honest, even though their tantrum may sound like they are dying, going to the gym daycare (or Grandma's house or wherever) for an hour is not going to kill them. And what would be different about the outcome if we would have followed through and gone to the gym? Mommy would be happy, mentally refreshed, and feeling good. Mommy wouldn't be at home sulking and binging on donuts. And, most assuredly, once the kids are picked up from the gym daycare, they will forgive and move on. Most probably they won't be scarred for life. And I could probably instantly win them back over by getting them ice cream on the way home. And we would all go home happy.

And I can't say all of this without also mentioning that this can go the other way too. If you are putting a boatload of pressure on yourself to get to the gym every freaking Saturday, this can backfire also. It's 100% okay to skip the gym when you want to and spend the time playing board games or eating ice cream with your kids. Seriously. If you and the kids feel stressed and pressured and cranky, then maybe forcing the whole gym thing isn't the best idea on that particular day. For real, it's all about figuring out what the heck works for you and your kids.

So, back to my earlier point. In the above example, what mommy do I want to be for my kids? What mommy do I want to be modeling for them? Do I want to be a cranky, ice cream binging, self-sacrificing, thinking-I-am-doing-the-right-thing mommy? Or do I want to be an exercised, happy, refreshed mommy who sometimes makes her kids slightly uncomfortable (by putting them in the gym daycare or dropping them at Aunt Gigi's house) because she knows that it is for the greater good? Do I want to be a mom who dumps her sulking, grouchy feelings on her kids because she didn't get to go to the gym? Or do I want to be a mom who, on occasion, honors her own needs because she knows it is best for everyone involved?

Before going any further, in case anyone is wondering, I do believe that, as parents, we ARE supposed to sacrifice for our kids. We ARE supposed to put their needs first. We ARE supposed to put them before us. And I don't want anyone thinking that I am suggesting otherwise. I believe that, as single moms, we sometimes go way too far with putting our kids "needs" first. I think we sometimes feel guilty or shameful about our situations and we try to make up for it by meeting our children's every need or going to extremes to keep them comfortable. I will be the first person to step up and say that I have a tendency to be wholly self-sacrificing and I am famous for attempting to overcompensate. I will pack on thirty pounds and go completely broke, all while just trying to keep my kids "comfortable."

Here's something I find comforting. In my own personal experience, when something seems to be best for my kids, it is 99.999% of the time also best for me. And vice versa. How can this possibly be? Well, here are a few examples. When I consider the fact that my kids should eat more vegetables, this is also a good idea for me. When I think that my kids will benefit from having chores around the house, this (obviously!) benefits me too. When I think it's best for my kids if I keep my mouth shut about that thing their dad did that pissed me off, well, this is best for me too. Why? Because, in the long run, I don't want to be a mom who negatively talks to my kids about their dad even though that's really freaking hard sometimes. And, believe it or not, spewing venom towards my ex is truly doing me no good. And, on the other hand, when I think that doing yoga to relax is a good idea for me, then, yes, my kids also benefit from that. When I decide that getting my body healthy is a great idea for me, my kids also benefit from this because they learn that taking care of your body is important.

My point here is that living a life that doesn't feel good to us is probably doing our kids no good. We owe it to our kids and ourselves to try our hardest to live a happy, fulfilled, loving life. We owe it to our kids to try to be the best versions of ourselves. We owe it to our kids to be the role models that they need.

So let's do it! Let's be happy. Let's be fulfilled. Let's not give up on our dreams. Let's keep pushing forward even when it hurts. Let's not get lost. Let's not forget who we are - for our kids AND ourselves.

Chapter 2:
Who do you want to be?

B efore I got divorced, I (mostly) had my life together. I was in good shape, I was overjoyed to be a mom to my two kids, and I had hobbies and somewhat of a social life. Sure, I was tired and overextended pretty often like most moms of young children, but it wasn't anything I couldn't handle. I volunteered at my kids' school. I found time to exercise. I spent any free time I had walking, or reading, or working on a hobby. I felt pretty good.

And then I got divorced. And my entire world collapsed. Every part of my life started spiraling downwards.

The end of my marriage was something that I had known was coming but was, nonetheless, painful and life-altering. As anyone who has been through a divorce knows, even when you believe the divorce is the best idea, it still hurts and you still grieve the loss of your life as you know it. You still have to process that all of the hopes and dreams you once held for a long, happy life with this person and your children, have now gone out the window. And you have to face the scary, unknown, oftentimes daunting future that lies ahead.

The first couple of years after the divorce, I am pretty sure I was mostly operating on denial, shock, and, quite frankly, adrenaline. There was drama, anger (okay, more like rage), and lots of chaos internally. I lost a good bit of weight (and I was already pretty small back then), didn't eat much, drank embarrassing amounts of caffeine, sometimes drank too much wine (oof), and probably looked like a deer caught in the headlights the majority of the time. I was flittering around like a cricket trying to (mostly unsuccessfully) manage all my new responsibilities. I was forgetful, wishy-washy, and, let's just say, it wasn't my best look.

And then, I guess, reality started to sink in. I started coming down from the initial adrenaline boost I was living off of. The bills started piling up. I was working three or four jobs at a time and exhausted. I failed at a couple of attempts at new relationships. I started comforting myself with food and gained a bunch of weight. I started hiding from the world. I quit saying yes to invites from friends. Most importantly, I was pouring every ounce of the little energy that I had left into trying to be the best mom to my kids. This was the start of heading into rock bottom for me. This was the start of the lowest point of my life.

When I was at the very bottom of rock bottom, I lost all hope. I was buried in debt. My house went into foreclosure. I was overweight and felt physically awful. I was depressed and filled with anxiety. I was so lonely and felt completely isolated. And, for the most part, I couldn't see a way out. I couldn't see how things could ever turn around and get better. It just felt like it was all too much and it felt like something I couldn't recover from. I was convinced that I would be alone forever and that I would be working a bunch of jobs until the end of time to make ends meet. I knew that I would never be happy again. I couldn't envision a brighter future. I felt hopeless.

This whole rock bottom time lasted a few years. During this time, it was one disappointment after the other for me. The bad luck and bad feelings just kept coming, one after the other. The only thing holding me together was my two kids and how much I love them.

Eventually, things slowly (very slowly) started getting better. And, you know what helped? As I said earlier, I began to try and visualize myself through my kids' eyes. I took a good look at what they might see and I realized that, no matter how hard, I had to make some changes. And, you know what else helped? I flipped things around and imagined that my daughter was in my position. I visualized my daughter as me. And my heart sank. I immediately felt my heart fill with compassion and love and empathy for ME.

And you know what? Here I am, several years later, writing this book. Here I am in a much better place. I am happy. I have turned things around financially. I have lost (some) weight and started taking care of my body again. I don't feel so lonely and isolated anymore. And, once again, I have hope for the future.

So, if you are feeling hopeless about your current situation, know this. There is hope. There is a bright future. There is happiness ahead. And good news! They say that the more challenging your struggle is, the bigger the reward. So, if you are majorly struggling right now, you can go ahead and get excited because big things are in your future.

When becoming a single mom, somewhere along the way, it's so easy to get lost. Loneliness sets in, or financial burdens start coming on, or home repairs start needing attention. Or maybe there's drama with your ex, awkward situations with your kids' stepmom, or kids throwing temper tantrums. Whatever the case may be, it is so easy to get swept away. It's so easy to get bogged down with worrying about your kids. It's so easy to lose hope.

Or maybe you are a single mom by choice. Perhaps you have chosen to take this journey alone through IVF or adoption or some other means. In this case, you may be spared the drama with the ex or the insecurity about the new stepmom, or the despair and depression of divorce. But this doesn't necessarily mean you are free from all struggles. You still are the only person there when the baby cries in the middle of the night. You are still the only person paying all of the bills. You still are the only person left to deal with the leaking roof. And so on and so on.

So, I am not sure where you are on your journey right now, but if you are reading this, I imagine that you believe your life could use a little redo. Maybe you're just looking for a bit of zest in your life or maybe you are deep in rock bottom and need a complete overhaul. Whatever your case may be, there is hope. You can build a full, happy life with your kids.

So, where to start? Well, the first step in figuring out the path to take is figuring out where you are going. Where do you want to go? What life do you want to build?

One way that I have found to help with figuring things out is to start by asking a million questions. All kinds of questions. So, that being said, I put together some questions for you. So take out a notebook or journal and write down your answers to the following questions. Or go ahead and write in this book. I am purposely leaving plenty of room for writing. This is going to get you headed on the path to where you want to go. And be 100% honest with your answers! This entire process will not work unless you are completely honest. No shame here, girl! Let's go.

Future life questions:

1. In a year from now, what would you like to be different?

2. What feelings would you use to describe your future life?

3. What characteristics would you use to describe yourself in a few years?

4. Where do you want to be living?

5. How would you describe your dream home?

6. How does your future body look?

7. How does your future body feel?

8. How does your future self spend her free time?

9. Do you see a romantic relationship in your future?

10. How would this romantic relationship look and feel?

11. What would "future you" be looking for in a partner?

12. How would "future you" be treated in your relationships?

13. What job would you like to be doing?

14. How much money would you like to be making?

15. How would your future self feel about money?

16. What kinds of things would you like to do with your kids in the future?

17. How do you envision your relationship with your kids in the future?

18. How do you envision yourself as a mom in the future?

19. Do you see yourself taking up any hobbies or activities in the future?

20. Do you see yourself starting a business or working from home or finding a different job?

21. What kind of hobbies does future you have?

22. What does a typical day look like for future you?

23. What kinds of foods does future you eat?

24. What kinds of clothes does future you wear?

25. How do you and your kids spend holidays in the future?

26. Can you form a vision in your mind of a future that makes you excited?

Honestly, these are just a few of a million questions we could ask ourselves to figure out where we want to go. And over time your answers may change. That's why it's a good idea to focus on the feelings of what you want and work out the rest of the details as you go.

Let me give you an example. Back in my rock bottom days, I knew that my dream for my future was to be my own boss, doing something that involved helping people in some way, making some money, giving lots of money away to causes important to me, and working when and how I wanted. I also had a constant idea in my head that I wanted to have a career that made me excited to get out of bed in the morning. My job at that time made me DREAD hearing the alarm go off. So, in my quest to start working on my dream, I went through three completely different small business ideas and each one failed. Then I started writing books. And that has turned out to be my dream job. So the specifics of how my dream would play out changed over time. But my goal remained the same consistently. To be my own boss, somehow offer help to others, make money, give money back, and love what I do. Bingo.

So, back to you. This is going to take a little work. You're going to really have to think about this. What does your future look like?

Okay, so let's get to work!

Action steps:

1. Take out a notebook or piece of paper or your journal and sit quietly. Really think about this. Think about the questions you answered above. And then think about the feelings that go along with those things. What does it FEEL like to be future you? How does your body look and feel? How do your relationships feel? How do your finances feel? And so on.

2. Write down what you would like your life to look like in one year, five years, ten years, and twenty years.

3. Make sure you address all aspects of your life such as your relationships, your home, your work, your body, your feelings, your health, your happiness, your goals, your hopes and dreams, your finances, etc.

4. Write down specifics when you know them but try to also focus more on the feelings you want to have. For example, I want to feel

financially free. I want to feel loved and I don't want to feel lonely. I want my kids to feel safe, loved, and filled with joy. I want to feel abundant. I want to feel well-rested and relaxed. I want to feel stress-free. I want to feel energetic and vibrant. I want to feel happy. I want to feel at peace with my kids' dad and stepmom. I want to have no drama in my life. I want to have time to pursue my hobbies. And so on and so on.

Okay, how was that? Feeling jazzed up and want to do a little more work? Fabulous! Here are some extra credit opportunities:

Bonus Points!

Major bonus points to you if you do any (or all!) of the following:

1. Close your eyes and sit quietly for just five minutes (or more!) every single day and focus only on your future life. Envision all of the feelings and characteristics that you just described above. Picture what it looks like. Feel what it feels like. Get completely swept away in dreaming about it. Even if you have to lock yourself in the bathroom and sit on the toilet to do it. :)

2. Make a practice of writing just a few lines in your journal every single day about your hopes and dreams and what you want your future to look like. Even if your only current hope is to make it through the day without having a breakdown. That counts!

3. Start trying to put together a cozy space in your house that is just for you and your hopes and dreams and good vibes. It would

be awesome if you had a whole room to yourself but even your bedside table will work. Make the space comforting and calming and inviting. Maybe put some pictures you like. Maybe an essential oil diffuser. Maybe a pretty candle. Whatever makes you FEEL good. This space is great for writing in your journal OR taking ten deep breaths before you hit send on that angry text to your ex. It's whatever. :)

Okay! So, have you figured out what you would like your future to look like? Great. Now let's get to work on building that future!

Chapter 3:
Getting your mind right

Confidence is what's up. This is where we have to start if we want anything else to work. We have to build our self-esteem and get rid of any yucky thoughts. We have to get into the right headspace and start upping our vibe. So, this is where we begin our work.

As I talked about earlier, when I first got divorced and became a single mom, I was a complete mess. My finances started falling apart. I started living paycheck to paycheck and slowly went broke. I won't go into all the details but it wasn't pretty. Let's just say that it involved past due bills, living off of student loans, payday loans (ugh), foreclosure, near bankruptcy, and more.

At one point, my kids and I had to move back in with my dad. Yep. And, needless to say, that was a major blow to my self-esteem. I felt like a forty-something-year-old failure.

I had about as much self-esteem as I had money. And I was incredibly ashamed of my situation. And you know what made it like nine billion times worse? My ex-husband was doing just fine. He was doing better than fine. And when he would shower the kids with gifts that I could never afford, I felt like a loser. I felt like a failure. I was struggling to come up with gas money and he was jetting off to Antigua. I mean I don't know if he was really jetting off to Antigua, but it sure felt like that. This was a major problem for my self-confidence.

And relationships? Ugh. Immediately following my divorce, I went through a short spurt of dating and a few relationships that were nothing less than disastrous. There was drama, unavailability, and much heartbreak. Sitting in a nice restaurant on an uncomfortable date with a guy texting the ENTIRE time. Yep, that was me. Talk about a confidence breaker. And, yet again, you know what else broke my confidence? My ex-husband had moved right on. Right on into a brand-spanking-new relationship. Like easy peasy, lemon squeezy. Ugh. That was really hard for me. I was unavailable, unsuccessful, and unhappy in my post-divorce relationships and he just breezed right into a brand new marriage. What on earth? My self-esteem took a major hit. I was confident that something was DEFINITELY very wrong with me.

And maybe harder than anything else on my self-confidence was the state of my body. After divorcing, my body and general well-being fell to the very bottom of my priority list. I wanted to spend every second with my kids so I quit exercising. I was broke so I was constantly stressed about money. I altogether stopped putting any effort into self-care. I essentially abandoned myself. And, worst of all, I gained thirty pounds. Holy moly. Needless to say, I felt AWFUL. I was miserable. I was physically uncomfortable, exhausted all the time, and ashamed of myself. So I basically became a hermit. I was too ashamed of myself to go out in public. Other than work, the grocery store, and my kids' school stuff, I pretty much stayed home. My self-esteem crumbled with every cookie I ate to quell my anxiety. It was horrible. And really sad.

I don't know your situation, but I would imagine that, even if you are not as badly off as I was, your self-esteem could use a little boost.

I have come up with a little quiz to see if you need a little makeover in the confidence department. It is by no means a scientific quiz. It's just my personal experience that, if you can't answer "yes" to most of these questions, you may need a little more self lovin'.

Just circle yes or no to the questions below and then add up your answers. The more "no" answers you get, well, the lower your self-esteem might be. But no worries, friend. I am here to boost that confidence of yours right back up.

So, let's try it out. Be completely honest! Remember, no shame here. We are all here to do the hard work to make our lives awesome.

Confidence quiz:

1. Do you eat relatively healthily and take care of yourself?
YES / NO

2. Do you practice self-care regularly?
YES / NO

3. Do you feel okay about your finances?
YES / NO

4. Are your relationships drama-free?
YES / NO

5. Do you have an amicable relationship with your kids' other parent?
YES / NO

6. Do you have healthy, supportive, and fun friendships?   YES / NO

7. Is your home a place that you love?
   YES / NO

8. Is your living situation stable?
   YES / NO

9. Do you like the way your body looks?
   YES / NO

10. Do you feel like you have put the past
    behind you? YES / NO

11. Do you feel like you have healed
    from your last relationship?
    YES / NO

12. Do you feel comfortable without
    being in a relationship? YES / NO

13. Do you feel hopeful about your
    future? YES / NO

14. Do you feel excited about your hopes and dreams? YES / NO

15. Do you feel proud of your life? YES / NO

16. Are you able to let silly stuff roll off your back?   YES / NO

17. Do you avoid relationships in which you are mistreated? YES / NO

18. Are you "available"? YES / NO

19. Do you blow off people who try to make you feel bad?   YES / NO

20. Do you avoid toxic people? YES / NO

21. Do you talk to yourself kindly?
YES / NO

22. Do you talk to others kindly?
YES / NO

23. Do you feel your feelings instead of eating or drinking or smoking them?
YES / NO

24. Do you know that you are not a bad person for having failed at past relationships?   YES / NO

25. Do you know, deep down inside, that you are not a less-than person because you are a single mom?   YES / NO

26. Do you know that you are completely worthy of any and everything you want?
YES / NO

27. Do you know that you are enough?
YES / NO

28. Do you know that you are
AMAZING? YES / NO

Total up your answers here:

YES_____ NO_____

Okay, how did it go? Lots of "no" answers? Just a few? None? All of them?? No worries. Remember, acknowledging is the first step.

Now that we may have realized that we want to do a little confidence work, where do we start? Well, there are probably a gazillion things we can do but we are going to start with working on our self-talk and then go from there. Let's get started.

First off, it's time to ditch the past. Oh yes. It's time to say sayonara to those old regrets and bad feelings. It really is. I have no idea what your personal situation is, but if you are anything like me, you are an expert at dwelling on the past. I, for one, have a history of holding on for dear life to regrets and shameful feelings about the past. I am an expert at replaying past events and beating myself up over them. And I am also an expert at replaying past events and wanting to beat other people up over them. Oof. But, honestly, where did that get me? Well, literally nowhere. If anything, it pushed me backwards not forwards towards my goals. I have learned (the hard way) that absolutely nothing good comes from dwelling on the past. And what's the point? It serves absolutely no purpose but to keep you depressed and feeling bad.

I know; I can hear some of you right now. "Oh, but you don't understand, I made these really bad choices so I need to keep beating myself up about it. I don't deserve to feel good." Well, friend, that's exactly what I told myself for years and I am here today to tell you to cut it out. Just stop. Seriously! Stop beating yourself up and dwelling on the past. Stop! The past is the past and there is no point in living there. So tell your past it can suck it and that you won't be entertaining it anymore.

Of course, I don't know what your past involved. Maybe you were cheated on, or ditched coldly, or ghosted. And I can hear you saying, "But you don't understand, I was treated so terribly and I am so angry and I can't get over it!!". Or maybe you were the one who did the cheating and the ditching coldly and the ghosting. And I can hear you saying, "But you don't understand, I am such an awful person and

I can't stop beating myself up and I never deserve to be happy again!!". Either way, I am here to say that staying stuck in the past benefits nobody. If you need to do some therapy or process your feelings or just be overcome with grief for a minute, then please do it! We ALL need a little therapy at some point. There is a massive difference between healthily processing our feelings while moving through grief and getting stuck there. Once you have done the processing, it's time to move forward - for you and the kids.

We ALL make mistakes. We ALL get treated like crap at some point. We ALL deserve to have a better and brighter future. And, again, let's think about your kids in this situation. If they were stuck in the past and beating themselves up or torturing themselves with anger about how they were wronged, what would you tell them to do?

I am absolutely not intending to dismiss or diminish the horrible things that you may have been through. Really. If anything, I am a HUGE believer in acknowledging and honoring how awful life can sometimes be. I don't believe that you can move forward in life until you DO acknowledge and honor your past. My point here is that, if you have done the acknowledging and honoring, its time for the train to leave the station. It's time to leave all of that behind.

What if you were never in a relationship with your children's father? What if there was never any drama, or fighting, or nasty breakups? What if, for whatever reason, they were just never in the picture? Well, then maybe you aren't stuck in the past. But, then again, maybe you are. Maybe you have some pesky negative feelings that just won't quit hanging around. Like fear or guilt or shame or whatever. Well, those need to go too so you can go ahead and jump on the bandwagon with everyone else and start moving forward.

Alright, let's go ahead and get started. Here is your action plan

Action steps:

1. Simply start by trying to notice the way you talk to yourself. Honestly, this takes a lot of practice and consistency. But it needs to be done. If you catch yourself talking rudely to yourself, just stop, take a few deep breaths, and tell your brain to shut the heck up. Seriously.

   This is going to sound loony toony, but try picturing yourself as a little girl. Or, better yet, picture your daughter. Would you talk to her like that? Would you shame her or make her feel bad about herself? Heck no! Then why on earth is it okay to talk to yourself like that? Like I said earlier, we ALL make mistakes. We ALL do stupid things. We ALL go through tough times. We ALL are imperfect. And guess what? The only way to move on to better days is to forgive yourself. You can't move forward to a better life if you are dragged continuously backward by thoughts of the past. So quit beating yourself up. It's not helping anybody. And you don't deserve it! Really!

2. Now that we've ditched the dirty self-talk, let's replace it with something much better. Let's start training our minds to talk to us kindly. Driving in your car? Great! That's the perfect time to remind yourself of all the reasons you are awesome. Drifting off to sleep at night? Sweet! That's the perfect time to remind yourself of what a good mom you are and how hard you are trying. Get my drift? Just put a little effort into putting some good thoughts into your mind and replacing those no-good, pesky negative thoughts.

    Let me just stop right here and say something. Do you even acknowledge how hard it is to be a freaking single mom? Do you know that you are a badass for waking up again and again and giving it your all? Do you know that you are so amazing just because you love your kids so stinking much? Please take a minute here and just think about this. Single moms are special. Single moms are determined, and strong, and would walk out in front of a bus to save their children. Single moms are hustlers. Single moms have hopes and dreams for their futures. Single moms bust their butts to give their kids everything they possibly can. Single moms, oftentimes, will completely sacrifice themselves for the sake of their kids. Single moms are, quite often, their children's heroes.

So I don't want to hear one more second of negative self-talk because NONE of it is true.

3. Okay, now that we've started getting our mind right, what about our body? It doesn't matter if your body is big or small, tall or short, green or red. What does matter? If you like it. If you feel comfortable in it. If you feel, at the very least, somewhat pretty walking into a room. So what can we do to improve our body love?

First, I am a huge fan of doing anything that makes your body feel good. Like, physically feel really good. I LOVE taking long walks in the sunshine and listening to good music or a good podcast. Whenever you have time, why not squeeze in a bubble bath. Or do some yoga. Whatever feels good. And don't even get me started on how awful stress is for your body. Heart attack anyone? Do absolutely anything you can to lower your stress levels. Deep breathe. Meditate. Scream. Whatever it takes. It literally could save your life. And, lastly, you want to know what cheap thing I do to boost my self-esteem almost instantly? Head over to the mall and buy myself some new underwear. I am not even kidding. Nothing feels fresher and more empowering and confidence-boosting than a cute new pair of undies. Even the five-dollar ones from Target.

4. Quit engaging in any drama in your life. Drama is guaranteed to make you feel bad about yourself. Cut out toxic relationships. Don't get entangled in questionable situations. Don't stick around if someone is treating you poorly. Not texting or calling you back? Goodbye! Talking down to you? So long! Making you feel bad about

yourself? Hasta la vista! This is a non-negotiable step in the process. The drama has to be kicked to the curb if you are going to live your best life.

5. Let the anger go. Really. It is poison. I know; I get it. You may have been cheated on, ditched, abused, and treated like dirt. You may have been entangled with the biggest narcissist in town. You may have walked in on your baby daddy having too much fun with the babysitter. And that is absolutely horrible. And I am seriously so, so sorry. Nobody should EVER be treated like that. It is heartbreaking and gut-wrenching. But....if you are still angry about it, you will never move forward into the bright future that is possible for you. Somehow, some way, you have to let it go. Anger will destroy you. Anger will ruin your life and will probably give you cancer or some other horrible health condition. And, when you really think about it, as long as you are still angry, the other person or people that did you wrong are winning. They are controlling you. And who in the heck wants that? Like

they say, the very best revenge is to move on and be happy. But, really, this isn't about revenge. This is about doing what is best for YOU. And your kids. And, seriously, nothing feels better than getting to the point where you have let it all go and you just don't give one flipping flip about any of it anymore. It's freedom. Here's the good news. At some point in time, you WILL move on. You WILL let go of all the anger. You WILL not give two flips about it anymore. So…why not make it happen sooner rather than later?

6. Put yourself out there. Go on a date. Sign up for a class. Join that gym. Register for a marathon. Go to dinner by yourself. Take your kids on a vacation. Ask for help when you need it. We'll talk more about this later, but, for now, start thinking of little things you have wanted to do that put you a little outside of your comfort zone.

Doing things that put you outside of your comfort zone is pretty much guaranteed to give you a pretty big   confidence boost. Sometimes, acting like you are more confident than you really are will give you a little more confidence. Try it.

7. Know that you are not alone. I mean, I don't know what your situation is, and you may very well be all alone, but what I mean is that somewhere out there are other single moms. Other single moms who feel all alone. Other single moms who feel like they can't go on another minute. Other single moms who are broke. Other single moms who have gained thirty pounds. Other single moms who have zero self-esteem. Other single moms who have been on a million awful dates. Other single moms who have also cried themselves to sleep wondering how they will take care of their kids. Other single moms who are barely hanging on. Other single moms that feel completely alone and isolated. And, you know what? We are all in this together. Even when we are alone.

So I want you to try this. When you are feeling down or anxious or afraid, close your eyes, take a deep breath, and envision the approximately 12 million other single moms in the United States alone standing beside you and cheering for you. Imagine that we are all right there rooting for you. Maybe like in the movie *Braveheart* when Mel Gibson is on the hilltop and all of his troops are right behind him on horseback? Remember that scene? They had his back. Well, sister, just know that all of us other single moms have your back. You are not alone.

Okay. How was that? Feeling like you're a few steps closer to being your own biggest cheerleader? Awesome. Again, if you're feeling like a rockstar and want to keep this train going, here are some additional cool ideas for boosting that confidence of yours:

Bonus points!

1. Head to the library and check out some self-help, self-improvement, or other positive vibe books. Anything that feels good to you. Feeding your brain with positivity really does help. And, seriously, think about it. Your mind is only so big. The more you fill it with positive, encouraging content, the less room there will be for negative, confidence draining slop.

   P.S.- at the end of this book, you will find a list of some of my all-time favorite books, videos, and more.

2. When you are driving in your car, listen to music that makes you feel good or listen to podcasts that make you feel good. Is cranking up some Lil Wayne guaranteed to make you feel nothing but amazeballs? Go for it!

3. Write positive affirmations in your journal. What does that mean? Make a practice of writing things in your journal such as: I am a resilient badass, even when my circumstances are tough. I am worthy of ALL the love. I am doing the best I can and being a single mom is freaking hard. I am STRONG. And so on. Just write whatever makes you feel good. I know this can be super awkward and weird, but, seriously, it can help. So, why not?

4. Search "motivational speeches" on YouTube. I know, kind of geeky. But I am not lying when I say that listening to some of these speeches has gotten me through some seriously dark times. And it definitely gave my confidence a little boost. Do yourself a giant favor and search YouTube for the speech by Ben Lionel Scott called "Your value." I have watched and listened to this maybe 432 gazillion times and it still gives me goosebumps. Sheesh.

5. Try to do at least one thing every week (or, preferably, every day!) that makes you feel

like a badass. Like what? Say no to that donut like a boss. Paint your toenails black. Don't respond to a toxic person's text. Run a mile. Hold yourself back from screaming at your kid. Organize your pantry. Whatever. Just do it.

6. Come up with a list of things that instantly make you feel good. What am I talking about? Well, here are some examples of things that immediately make me feel good. Taking five slow, deep breaths. Sniffing essential oils or anything that smells good. Going outside. Meditating for five minutes. Standing in the sunshine and soaking up the warmth for sixty seconds. Listening to "Let It Be" by The Beatles. Get it? Okay, so these will be your little go-to tricks for when you are feeling really freaking stressed or really freaking bad. Just something quick, easy, and free that instantly boosts your mood.

How do you feel now? Have some ideas for how you are going to build up your self-confidence? Awesome. Let's keep going.

Wait, I thought of one more thing. Before we move on, I want to just note something that I think is felt by a lot of single moms. Sometimes it seems like there is a stigma about being a single mom. Think about any movies you may have seen where there is a single mom character. What did you see? Often, the single mom character is portrayed as a broke, exhausted, hustling, bitter person who is barely surviving. And look, I get it; that is precisely how it is a lot of the time. That was a perfect description of me several years ago. And I was miserable. And I had literally zero confidence.

Here's an example. Remember the movie *The First Wives Club*? If you do, think back to how the "first wives" were portrayed. For the most part they were bitter, jealous, revenge-obsessed, frumpy, sad, and just all-around no fun. And the thing is, unfortunately, that's how it can be. I was like this for more than a minute. I had my moments that I now cringe when I think about them. I went through a period of rage and bitterness. I felt that I looked just like the quintessential frumpy ex-wife. Ugh. And just thinking about myself like this zapped every ounce of self-esteem I had.

What I want to say here is that, it's okay and 100% normal to go through this. But, what we want to avoid is getting stuck there. Or feeling like that is our identity. Just because that's how it looks in movies does not mean that that's how it has to be for us. And if you are going through this right now, I want you to know that it doesn't last forever. I know, because I have been there and come out on the other side.

A lot of times, it seems that our level of self-esteem is directly correlated to how we perceive that our life is going. If everything appears to be going great and we are feeling abundant, we often have abundant levels of self-esteem. If it feels like everything is falling apart and we feel broke and like nothing is working out, we often have zero self-esteem. So the good news is that, when we work on elevating different areas of our lives, our self-esteem usually gets boosted along the way.

So let's get to work on raising our vibes. Let's ditch the negative self-talk. Let's start acknowledging how much we have been through and how strong we are. Let's remember that we are worthy. Let's not forget that we are single moms and that, in and of itself, means that we are pretty freaking awesome.

Chapter 4:
Feeling good

Self-care. What on Earth is that? Yep, I know. It's probably something many of us single moms have never heard of, some foreign concept that doesn't apply to us. Between getting our kids to bed, working two jobs, and trying to fix the washing machine, there's not much time left for anything else.

Before I became a single mom, I had a bit of me-time. On occasion, when my then-husband would be watching the kids, I could run to the grocery alone (aahhh), or get a haircut alone, or just take a long bubble bath without worrying that my kids might burn down the house while I soaked in the lavender suds.

And then I got divorced and all that went out the window. No more solo trips to the grocery. No more long soaks in the bubble bath. No more help with fixing the broken garbage disposal. No more help with paying the bills. No more me time.

Yes, when I got divorced, my kids did start spending every other weekend with their dad. So, yes, I technically had every other weekend free to myself. I could have spent the forty-eight hours soaking in the tub, watching Netflix, and browsing the grocery store aisles in peace. But, you know what I did? Instead of relishing the alone time and using it to recharge my batteries, I used the time to pick up extra shifts at work. Or I hung out with toxic friends or boyfriends because I didn't want to be alone. Or I feverishly cleaned the house, mowed the lawn, and did home repairs until I was utterly exhausted.

Looking back, I know that I did all of these things because I missed my kids so terribly much and I was doing any and everything I could to avoid thinking about missing them. I was "keeping busy" and avoiding sitting still and acknowledging how empty and alone I felt. Plus, I wanted to get as much work and as many chores done as physically possible so that, when they came home, I would have more "free time" to spend with them.

Well, this didn't work out too well. I remained constantly stressed. I never felt recharged. And I can say, without a doubt, filling your time with toxic people to avoid being alone never works out well.

Eventually, I started realizing what I was doing and I made myself slow down. And, to be honest, it felt horrible at first. When I slowed down, I was forced to realize how I was feeling and acknowledge how sad and lonely I was. And that didn't feel good. But, I realize now that I just needed to feel those feelings for a while and then they went away. I started relaxing more on the weekends. I made myself go to movies by myself, which, to be honest, felt really freaking awkward and weird. But I realized that doing that was better than sitting home alone and being miserable. And it was way better than going with a toxic person just so that I didn't have to go alone.

Anyway, after some time, I got the hang of being a more chill person during my alone time and it felt amazing. I started meditating. I started going for walks in the sunshine. I started watching Netflix and reading good books. I quit working excessively on my alone weekends. I dedicated this time to taking care of me, even when I kept feeling like I "should" be doing something else like working or cleaning.

If you are a single mom with no help at all and your children's father is not in the picture, I don't even know what to say. I cannot even imagine. I feel so strongly for you and, if I could, I would come to your house and watch your kids for a day for you so that you could have some freaking alone time. I don't even know how you manage. But all my good vibes are headed your way. I am hoping there is some resource out there that can help you out a bit with childcare or babysitting or house cleaning or something. I really, really hope so.

Okay, so the point of this chapter is to talk about self-care and feeling good. You may be thinking I am talking about going to the spa or eating healthy or something else typically classified as self-care. And, yes, I am talking about those things. But, I am also talking about other things that sometimes get forgotten but are so important to self-care. Like setting good boundaries. Like saying no when you mean no. Like avoiding abandoning yourself in order to please others. Yep, those all fall under self-care.

Okay, so let's get started with a quiz. Same as always, the more "no" answers you have the more self-care work we need to do. No big deal, we've got this. Here we go.

Self care quiz:

1. Do you have any alone time?
   YES / NO

2. Do you ever "relax"? YES / NO

3. Do you ever treat yourself to something special like a manicure or take the day off from doing laundry to watch a movie? YES / NO

4. Do you try to eat nutritious foods? YES / NO

5. Do you try to move your body regularly? YES / NO

6. Do you meditate or do some other form of breath work or mind-clearing? YES / NO

7. Do you feel peaceful for the most part?   YES / NO

8. Do you feel rested?   YES / NO

9. Do you spend any time doing adult things like hanging out with friends or going to a concert or something else that doesn't involve kids? YES / NO

10. Do you regularly make time for yourself without feeling guilty about it?   YES / NO

11. Do you say no to things you want to say no to? YES / NO

12. Do you go to the doctor when you need to and do other things to nurture your health?
YES / NO

13. Do you avoid toxic situations and people? YES / NO

14. Do you try to avoid negative self-talk? YES / NO

15. Do you treat yourself with the same compassion and care that you give to your kids?
YES / NO

16. Do you avoid drama?
YES / NO

17. Do you have a list of at least five things that can instantly boost your mood? YES / NO

18. Do you not tolerate bad behavior from people you are dating and others? YES / NO

19. Do you speak up for your needs and wants in all of your relationships? YES / NO

20. Do you avoid codependent behavior such as people-pleasing and acting like a doormat? YES / NO

21. Do you feel like you have released the "baggage" from your past? YES / NO

22. Do you feel happy, nurtured, and ready for a bright future? YES / NO

Total up your answers here:

YES_____   NO_____

Okay, so how did that go? Remember, no need to get concerned if you just marked every answer with a no. That's what we're here for. To turn your "nos" into "yeses"!

Alright, let's go ahead and dive right into the self-care action steps.

Action steps:

1. Let's start with taking out our journal and writing down areas of your life that you are not pleased with. Maybe things you regularly that you dread or do only out of "obligation."

    For example, do you cram your alone time with work or chores or hanging out with people you don't really even like? Would you prefer to spend your one night alone taking a bubble bath and reading that new book you just bought but, instead, you feel obligated to hang out with your friends because that's the only time you can do it? Maybe you hate drinking but you do it because everyone else is and it's the social expectation, even though it makes you feel sick and unhealthy? Maybe you hate that your kids have talked you into buying Chick-fil-A every afternoon but, even though it's making you broke and you know it's probably not the healthiest thing, you keep doing it so that your kids are "happy"? Well, this is the point in time where we talk about setting boundaries.

In my own experience, boundaries require a lot of courage, strength, and determination. It can be really freaking hard to say, "No," sometimes. But, as I have learned (the hard way), sometimes you have to say no matter how hard it seems. One of my very favorite quotes is by a woman named Maggie Kuhn. She said, "Stand before the people you fear and speak your mind – even if your voice shakes." Phew, if that ain't the truth.

Let me give you a quick example. Several years ago, I had a friend that frequently asked me to do things for her. Maybe run an errand. Maybe babysit her child so she could get to work on time. Maybe cover for her when she needed an excuse to not be at a party. Eventually, it occurred to me that I was more of a personal assistant than a friend. I realized that I needed to say no to her. And that terrified me. I was at the point where I didn't want to be the person with no friends. So, I was willing to do almost anything to keep the friends I had. And this included abandoning myself in order to please her. So, I waited nervously for the next time she would text and ask me for a favor. And, when she did, it took all the courage I had, but I said no. My hands shook as I hit send on the text, but I did it. And, you know what? I didn't die. My life didn't end. And she didn't fire back an angry text and tell me I was a horrible person. She just said, "K." My guess is that she texted another "friend" and got them to do the favor for her. Anyway, the most important thing is that I got my courage back. I was proud of myself. I stuck up for ME and lived to tell about it.

In what areas of your life do you need to speak your mind? Who or what do you need to say no to? Saying no can be one of the most freeing things you will EVER do. And it is truly a huge part of self-care. When you set boundaries and say no to things that are not good for you, you honor yourself. And when you don't set boundaries and say yes when you really mean no, you are abandoning yourself. And remember, doing the right thing for you is almost always the right thing for your kids also! And if you feel scared when you go to tell someone or something, "No," just remember to envision your single mom tribe standing beside you like Mel Gibson in *Braveheart*; rooting for you and cheering you on. You CAN do it.

2. Since we have now talked about the importance of saying no, let's talk about saying yes! What in your life have you been saying no to that you really want to say yes to? For example, maybe you got asked on a date but, you say no because you feel guilty about leaving your kids even though you might want to go. Or maybe you really think it would be a wonderful experience for your kids to see the Grand Canyon, but you cave and take them to Disneyworld every single summer because that's where they want to go. Or maybe you really, really want to apply for that job you always wanted but you don't because you are scared of making a change. Whatever the case may be, in which areas do you want to start saying yes more? Honestly, saying yes can be just as scary as

saying no. But it can also be just as freeing and self-loving as saying no.

Here's an example of how hard saying yes can be but also how beneficial and important it can be. Think back to earlier when I talked about my dilemma of whether or not to go to the gym. I desperately wanted (and needed) to go to the gym for just one hour. But my kids did not want to go and threw a tantrum about it. What if I said yes to my needs instead of saying no in order to please them? What if I knew they would be perfectly fine in the gym daycare and that, even though dragging them to the gym would feel like absolute hell, it would be worth it to say yes to myself and do it. Me saying yes to my needs in this situation would be good and healthy for all of us because, in the end, my kids would see that mommy needs to occasionally take care of herself and also that we all need to take care of and honor our bodies.

3. Now that we are all about saying yes and no when we want to, let's work on adding in

some good feelings. What do you do to feel good? Do you ever make time for yourself? Do you have any routines or rituals that make you feel calm and centered? Do you spend any time working on your hopes and dreams? Do you have any hobbies that you let yourself enjoy? Well, if you didn't answer yes to any of those questions, let's get to work on making some changes.

You see, when you make time for yourself, you are telling the universe that you are important. When you give yourself permission to prioritize yourself from time to time, you are honoring yourself. And that is self-love.

So what can you do today to start honoring yourself and showing the universe that you matter? Do you need to get a babysitter for one hour one day a week so that you can go to the library and research your dream job? Do you need to tell your kids no to McDonald's this afternoon so that you can use that fifteen dollars to buy that book you've wanted about how to build a vegetable garden? Do you need to ask your mom if she can watch your baby for one weekend so that you can get some freaking sleep and go for long walks in the sunshine and regain your sanity? Whatever it may be, give yourself permission to make yourself a priority every once in a while.

4. Lastly, it seems to me that how we take care of ourselves and our bodies is usually a direct reflection of how much we love ourselves. If you put horrible things into your body and mind, you probably could work on your self-love a little bit. When we truly love ourselves, it comes automatically to want to take care of ourselves.

    So what are you regularly feeding your body and mind? Do you eat pizza and donuts all day and watch the real housewives of wherever all night? Do you smoke or drink a lot and hang around super negative people who ooze bad vibes? Do you use drugs and spend your days fighting with your ex through texts?

Listen, I am absolutely not judging a single thing anyone does. Believe me when I say that I have done my share of all of the above. Ugh. But what I know (from my own experience) is that, when you are doing these things, there is no way you really love yourself. And that needs to change. You are so worth it. You are so deserving of real self-love and real self-care. So, take a look at what you are putting into your mind and your body. Then, see what needs to change.

Real self-care looks like feeding yourself (most of the time) nourishing, healthy foods. Real self-care looks like feeding your mind with positivity. Real self-care looks like saying no to smoking, drugs, and heavy drinking. Real self-care looks like saying no to toxic people and situations. Real self-care looks like having the courage to make the scary leap of letting go of the past. All of this can be really hard. And it requires effort. But it is so worth it. YOU are so worth it.

Okay, how are we feeling? Feeling ready to start doing a little more caring for YOU? Yes!

Alright go-getters. If you want to take it a step further, here's your chance. Up next are your bonus point activities.

<u>Bonus Points</u>!

1. Think of little things you can do throughout the day to practice self-care. Maybe try your hardest to put your phone down and pick up that self-help book. Maybe choose to have an apple after lunch instead of a cookie. Maybe try your hardest not to drink eight million Diet Cokes like I used to. Ugh. Maybe choose to give deep breathing a try, even just for two minutes before you respond to that infuriating text. And this may sound super woo woo, but when you do each of these little things, stop and tell yourself that you are doing it because you love you. Better yet, look in the mirror and say out loud to yourself, "YOU are so loved and you are such a badass because today you are choosing this healthy apple over these delicious-looking cookies and that means that you are basically a goddess!" I know; it's weird. But whatever. Who really cares?! And, honestly, sometimes it works for me and sometimes I have zero patience for that

craziness and I eat the entire plate of cookies. Oof.

2. If possible, plan a day just for you. I know this is hard logistically and mentally but give it a try. It can be months away. Find someone to watch your kids. Request time off from work. Say no to ALL responsibilities for the day. Plan a day full of things you wouldn't normally get to do. If you can afford it, go somewhere. Drive to the beach. Fly to a fun city. Check into a hotel for the night. Get a massage. Go shopping. Go for a long stroll in the sun. Pamper yourself. It doesn't even have to cost money! Just take the damn day off and don't do anything related to being a mom. No housework. No cleaning. No grocery shopping. Just pure YOU time. Go for a long bike ride and then take a bubble bath and then go to the library and check out some new books. Sign up for a free class on watercolor painting at your local college or library. Go day drinking if you want to. Whatever floats your boat and lets you relax. Let it all freaking go. Everyone needs a day

off from all responsibility every once in a while.

So, what can you do today to start caring for yourself? You really are SO worth it! Don't forget that you are showing your kids how to take care of themselves by taking care of yourself. And that equals a happy momma and happy kids.

Chapter 5:
Relationships

The next stop on this journey to our best life is to take a good, long look at our relationships. All of our relationships. Yes ma'am. With friends, family, and partners. With our kids, our exes, our co-workers. All of them. Past, present, and future.

Oh yeah, you heard me right. We are going to have to take a look at the past, but only because we need to figure out what hasn't worked for us before so that we can figure out what will work for us in the future. And, look, nobody said building an incredible life was going to be easy. It's going to take some hard work. But we can totally do it.

So let's start by taking just a few minutes to look back on our past romantic (or maybe not so romantic) relationships. Think back to how each of your relationships played out. How did your relationships start? What were they like while they lasted? Was there a lot of drama? Was there a lot of joy? Did you feel good about yourself in these relationships? Did you feel unhappy or mistreated? How did the relationships end? Do you notice any similarities between the relationships?

Next, let's take a minute and think about our relationships with our kids. Do you feel like there are any areas you would like to work on to build a better relationship with your kids?

What about your family? Do you have any toxic family members you may need to distance yourself from? Do you have consistently healthy, mutually respectful relationships that you treasure? Do you have anyone you would really like to make amends with?

What about your job? Do you get along with your co-workers? Do you often get into power struggles with your co-workers? Do you love your bosses and feel great about your relationships? Do you have that one co-worker who you just can't seem to jive with?

And since this is a book for single moms, I would imagine that there is a good chance there might be another woman in your children's lives. Is your ex remarried? Does he have a girlfriend? A boyfriend? No matter the case, this is an area that can be so stinking HARD. I make jokes here and there about wishing a spaceship would swoop down and pick up my kids' stepmom but, the truth is, for a good while I was not joking. As they say, I have come a long way baby. But at first, I was jealous, possessive, and wanted nothing to do with the idea of another woman coming anywhere near my kids. I didn't even know this person but I was convinced that she needed a punch in the throat. How dare she take my daughter to the mall when my kids went to their dad's house for the weekend? How dare she make my son mouth-watering apple pie after school? And the nerve of her to buy my kids birthday presents!! No joke, these were some of my true feelings at the beginning. But the fact of the matter was that I was scared. I was scared my kids would love this woman more than me. I was afraid my kids would want to spend more time with her. I was scared they would run to her for comfort, instead of me, when they had a bad day. And all of those scenarios felt utterly soul-crushing to me.

Eventually, I came to realize that no matter what, my kids will always love me and call me momma. And the most important thing is that my kids are treated well and loved. And I reminded myself to remember to take a look at who I wanted to be in this situation. What kind of person do I want my kids to see me be in this situation? An angry, dramatic, jealous, unaccepting person? Or a person who is able to put her (mostly unfounded) fears aside for the sake of her kids?

Anyway, if you are dealing with "the other woman" in your kids' lives, I am sending you good vibes and courage for the journey. Because this road can be majorly bumpy.

And lastly, but certainly not least, what about your friends? Do you feel supported and loved by them? Do you even like them? Do they help to bring out the best in you and cheer you on along your journey? Or do they ooze negativity and bring you down every time you interact with them?

Okay, now that you have done a little thinking about your relationships, what do you see? Look, there is nooooo shame here. I mean I for one am guilty of not having the best relationship track record. And I am super guilty of some cringe-worthy embarrassing moments in my past. Eek.

Let me give you an example. Even though this is thoroughly embarrassing to talk about, I am hoping it will make you feel not so different if you have had a few relationship blips. Okay, I'll just start by saying that I have sent multiple "accidental" texts to a guy when I hadn't heard from him. I have creepily driven by a guy's house when he said he wasn't home to see if he was lying or not. I have passive-aggressively told my boss that I didn't hear my phone ringing when she called me to ask me to do something. I have tried to keep my kids all to myself and minimize the time they spend with their dad. I have prolonged relationships that I knew were not going to work out just so that I wouldn't be alone. I have continued to hang out with toxic friends because I didn't want to have "no friends." I have wished (several times) that an alien spaceship would come down to earth and take my kids' stepmom to Mars. Yikes.

I could go on for days and days. The point is my past relationships have definitely left something to be desired. I could have chosen better people. And, even though I hate to admit it, I could have been a much better person. Ouch.

But that's the past! We are here today to work on our future. And our future relationships can be dramatically better if that's what we want.

I want to stop here quickly and mention that this is where the importance of building our confidence and practicing self-care comes in, especially when it comes to romantic relationships. I would argue that, if your confidence is low and you are not taking care of yourself, you are 100% not ready for a meaningful long-term relationship. If your confidence is low, you will often accept treatment that is less than you deserve.

When I first started dating after getting divorced, I literally had zero self-esteem, my life was a mess, and I had completely quit taking care of myself. And you know what happened? I tolerated guys that wouldn't text me back. I tolerated guys that didn't call. I tolerated relationships that left me feeling horrible. I have literally lived through dates where, while sitting at the dinner table in a fancy restaurant, I watched my date STARE at the cute, young waitress the entire night. And I said nothing and continued to date the darn guy because I didn't want to fail at another relationship. And I was convinced that that was all I deserved.

So, if you find yourself still putting up with guys or girls that don't text you back, or guys or girls that mistreat you, please go back and reread the chapters on confidence and self-care. No worries, this process takes time and sometimes we need a LOT of practice. Lord knows I have.

Anyway, if you are not happy in your current relationships, you cannot keep doing whatever you have been doing. New things require new ways of doing.

Before we take our next quiz, I want to talk about the importance of "finding your tribe." I am going to talk about it more in a minute, but I want to give you an example of what this has meant to me. For a long time, I have heard people say how important it is to "find your tribe". I never really thought about it before, assumed it meant that you should hang around people you like and that support you. Right? Well, as time has gone by, I have really started to understand what this means to me, personally. I would now define "finding your tribe" as intentionally hanging around people who make you feel most like yourself. People who bring out the "you" in you. In the most happiest way.

Let me give you an example:

As far as nursing goes, there are like a gazillion different jobs/specialties/careers that you can choose from. For instance, school nurse, home health nurse, legal nurse, ER nurse, dialysis nurse, nurse educator, etc., etc., etc. Well, through my own experience, I have found that these different nursing specialties often attract different types of nurses. Not to generalize people, but just to say that (in my experience!) the nurses that work in case management are often slightly different, personality-wise, than the nurses that work the night shift in the ER. These differences are neither good nor bad; they're just different. It's the same idea as thinking that you would PROBABLY find a different group of people at a quilting convention versus a Motley Crue concert. But I don't know, maybe not! Anyway, my point is, different types of people flock to different kinds of things. And none of these preferences make them good or bad people. Just different.

Okay, so back to what I am trying to explain. For years I worked in nursing jobs where, for the most part, I enjoyed my job but there was always something slightly off. I really liked the other nurses I worked with but there was always a little something nagging in the back of my mind that told me that these were not my people. It's like they were friendly and they were funny and they were great nurses, but there was something just slightly off. Like maybe they didn't think the same way I did or something. Maybe like going on a first date with a guy and they are nice and funny and probably look great on paper, but there is just zero spark there.

Well, after years of working in different nursing positions I started a new job with a new specialty. And, guess what? I found my tribe! I instantly had an internal sense that I could relax around these people and be 100% myself. I felt more "me" than I had in a long, long time. It's almost like these people brought out the "me" in me. And, man oh man, did that feel good.

You can apply this to all the people in your life and start paying attention to who you really feel like you can be your authentic self around. Do you have people in your life who you feel you need to edit yourself around? Are you dating a guy who you don't feel comfortable being your whole self around? Do you often feel the need to keep your honest feelings to yourself around certain people? If you find yourself nervous or uncomfortable around people or like you have to be "someone else" around them, these probably aren't your people.

My point is that finding your tribe is so freeing. Finding your tribe can do wonders for your self-esteem and your happiness. I have found that when I hang around people who are not my tribe kind of people, my self-esteem drops. I start to feel like something is wrong with me. But there's not actually anything wrong with me; it's just that I am hanging around people who aren't meant for me. Anyway, I can't even tell you how important I think it is to seriously find your tribe.

Okay, it's quiz time! Same as before. The more "no" answers you have the more work we need to do to build the relationships we want. And that's okay! It all starts with figuring these things out. Here we go:

Relationships quiz:

1. Do you genuinely feel like you have happy and healthy relationships? YES / NO

2. Do you feel like you have all the relationships you want? YES / NO

3. Do you feel safe in your relationships? YES / NO

4. Do you feel like your relationships are mutually respectful? YES / NO

5. Do you feel trusted and trusting in your relationships? YES / NO

6. Do you avoid relationships with drama? YES / NO

7. Are your relationships easygoing and fun? YES / NO

8. Do you feel like you have people that you can rely on? YES / NO

9. Do you feel good about your relationship with your kids?
YES / NO

10. Are your relationships mostly conflict-free? YES / NO

11. Has it been a good while since you had a big fight with someone?
YES / NO

12. Has it been a long while since someone treated you poorly?
YES / NO

13. Has it been a good while since you put up with things like not returning texts, lying, and other dramatic stuff? YES / NO

14. Are you open and honest in your relationships? YES / NO

15. Do you avoid engaging in power struggles and passive aggression? YES / NO

16. Do you have a decent relationship with your children's father? YES / NO

17. If your children's father has a new partner, are you on good terms with them or, at least, not actively engaged in drama with them? YES / NO

18. Do you have a positive view of love?
    YES / NO

19. Do you know that you are worthy of great relationships and being treated well? YES / NO

20. Do you believe that you deserve love? YES / NO

21. When you hang around the people in your life, do you feel like YOU?
    YES / NO

22. Do you feel like you have found your tribe? YES / NO

Total up your answers here:

YES_____   NO_____

So let's get started daydreaming about what we want our future relationships to look like. And after we figure out what we want them to look like, let's start figuring out how to build them. Are you ready? Let's go.

Action steps:

1. Take out your notebook or journal. Make a general list of all the relationships you plan to have in your life in the future. For example, your kids, a romantic partner, your family, your co-workers, your friends, etc.

2. Under each relationship category, write down at least five characteristics that you would like each of these relationships to have. For example, if thinking of my kids, I might write down: honesty, fun, affection, traveling together, and laughing. When I write down my friends, I might write: feeling and giving loving support, laughing, vulnerability, companionship, and fun. When I write down a romantic partner, I might write: feeling and giving love, happiness, feeling safe, companionship, romance. And so on and so on.

3. Now, under each of these categories, after you consider the qualities you want to have

in the future, you need to write down at least five things that you can do to work towards these relationship goals. Okay, this is going to take some work. So let me give you a few personal examples of what this may look like.

Do you want to be at peace with your kids' dad? I get it; sometimes this can seem like it's never going to happen. But it really can! So, maybe today you can just commit to not responding to any negative texts you get. Or maybe you can commit to not sending any negative texts. I know, I know. It can be really hard! Maybe you can be super generous and let your kids stay an extra few hours with their dad. Or maybe you can commit to being friendly to your kids' new stepmom at the school play or, at the very least, not grabbing her by the hair and taking her out back.

Or, if you want to work towards having a new husband (or wife!) one day, start embodying the qualities you want your future man to have. Want him to be loving?

Then be loving. To your kids or the neighbor or your cat or whoever. Want him to be fully available? Then you need to be fully available. No more drama with the ex or hiding your feelings or being flaky. Want him to be generous? Then you be generous. Give a few dollars to your favorite charity or buy your friend lunch or whatever. Just start working on being the person you hope to attract. And, honestly, this applies to all the relationships in your life. Not just future Prince Charming.

4. Hang around good people. Have you ever heard that quote by Jim Rohn that says, "You're the average of the five people you spend the most time with"? Well, I guess it's probably true. So take a look at the people you hang out with the most. What do you see? Do you like them? Do you like their potential futures? Are they headed where you are headed?

For example, are you hoping to become a health coach but all your friends are unhealthy, addicted to food or drugs or drinking and spend their days whining? Or are you daydreaming about starting your own business but your friends and family all sit around watching Netflix while telling you that you will never be successful?

A few years back, I heard this quote and figured that I was screwed. Yikes. I had a dilemma. My dilemma was that, if I cut out people who were not good for me, then there wouldn't be very many people left in my life. And I didn't believe that was a good idea. I thought I would be even more of a failure if I cut out toxic friends and was left with zero close friends. So, I stuck with the toxic friendships. And then, I heard a couple of powerful things that really hit home with me.

First, I heard that, when you have the courage to release the wrong people, the right people will show up. You just have to trust and be willing to be alone for a bit.

And second, I heard that it's okay if your tribe is temporarily people you have never met. What?? Yep. It's okay if your tribe is temporarily podcast hosts, self-help and motivational book authors, motivational and educational speakers, characters on TV that you can relate to, etc. If these people you have never met are better for your self-esteem than your own darn friends, then it's totally okay to say goodbye to your real-life friends and say hello to your radio/TV/book friends. And, in due time, the right real-life friends will show up. And they will be worth the wait.

5. Start paying attention to how you act in your current relationships. Are you a good friend? Do you treat people with respect? Do you take the time to listen when your child really wants to tell you something? Do you show vulnerability and form close bonds with people? All of these things can be important in relationships, so it never hurts to just spend some time thinking about our own behavior and anything we can improve on.

6. Lastly, think again about how you envision your best self. Think again about the example you are setting for your babies.

What kind of person do you want to see? What kind of person do you want your kids to see? Do you want to be the friend who always has a minute to listen? Do you want to be the mom who tells her kids every day how proud she is of them? Do you want to be the girlfriend who doesn't flip her lid when her boyfriend occasionally wants to have a night out with the boys? Do you want to be the kind of co-worker who always helps her teammates when needed? Do you someday want to be the grandma who all the grandkids love to spend time with?

Once you have considered the person you want to be, then start acting like her! Start playing the role of the woman of your dreams. Start getting out of bed in the morning with the attitude of the amazing woman that you truly are.

Okay, how was that? Got some ideas for how you can do a little tweaking in the relationships department? Perfect! And, as usual, here are some extra activities if you want to do a little more:

<u>Bonus Points!</u>

1. I have only one bonus point activity here but it's SUPER important. Are you ready? Find yourself some single moms!!!

    In any way, shape, or form! Online, in your town, on social media, wherever. It really doesn't matter. Just find some. Why? Because this can be one of the most empowering things you can do as a single mom.

    When I first became a single mom, I didn't know any other single moms in my small town. I felt completely alone and I felt 100% DIFFERENT than every other mom in town. I felt like there was something very wrong with me.

    One day, I stumbled upon a single mom group on Facebook. And my eyes literally lit up because these women were speaking my language! They were talking about feeling lonely. They were talking about feeling overwhelmed with responsibilities. They were talking about struggling to pay the bills. They were talking about wanting to poke their kids' stepmom's eyes out. And I was thrilled!! This was like music to my ears! I felt more understood, free, and NOT alone than I had in years. And it was so incredibly empowering. I no longer felt like an alien on this Earth.

When you connect with others that are going through some of the same circumstances as you, you can feel empowered, understood, heard, and seen. And this is so unbelievably good for you. This can boost your self-esteem like eight bazillion notches and really give you some seriously strong feelings of validation. And, Lord Jesus, if we don't all need that sometimes. Phew.

There are Facebook groups for single moms (I just started one and I would LOVE to have you! Just search Single Moms Building Big Lives group on Facebook or go to my website and there's a link). There are

Instagram accounts for single moms. There are websites and books for single mommas. And of course, some real-life single moms who may be living down the street from you.

However you do it is fine. I just can't recommend enough that you get yourself some single mommas. You don't have to be best friends or anything. Just seek out some single moms so that you know you are not alone.

Okay, got some juices flowing in the relationships department? Awesome!

As we all know, relationships can be hard. And some are going to come and go. And that's totally okay. All we can do is work to be our best selves and a good momma to our kids. The rest will work itself out. And, hopefully, along the way we will find our tribes.

Chapter 6:
Bringing home the bacon

F irst of all, me trying to give out
financial advice might be like the
blind leading the blind. Let me

just start by giving you a vision of where I was several years ago. I hated my job. I was broke. I was constantly stressed about money. I felt hopeless about my bleak financial future. I was severely discouraged by the idea of having to work four jobs for the rest of my life to make ends meet. I was living off of student loans. My house went into foreclosure. I met with a bankruptcy attorney. I was at rock bottom. Phew.

With lots of hard work, lots of crying, and lots of embarrassment, I've made a bit of progress since then. Thank God. That was probably one of the worst times of my life. Nothing is more stressful (well, maybe a few things) than financial problems. Nothing is scarier than your car breaking down when you have no money. Nothing sucks more than suffering day after day at a job that you hate. And nothing will make you panic more than not knowing how you will feed your kids.

I don't know about you, but I see bigger and better things for myself than living the rest of my life paycheck to paycheck. And I really want to be doing work that I love. I want it to not feel like work. And I really want to live financially comfortably.

What about you? Do you love your job? If not, do you have some sort of vision for a future job? Do you feel financially comfortable? Do you have goals for your finances?

Now look, I am going to go ahead and say it. If your goal is to find a sugar daddy and let him worry about the money, then more power to you! But.....what if an alien spaceship comes down to Earth and carries all the men away in it? Then what? Well, we better have a plan B in place. Just in case.

I am going to assume that you want to do a little work in this area so let's just go ahead and jump right in. You know how the quizzes work! The more "no" answers you have, the more work we need to do in this department. And don't forget, honesty is key. No shame or judgement coming from me!

Job and finances quiz:

1. Do you feel financially stable?
   YES / NO

2. Do you have a little cushion of savings? YES / NO

3. Are you pretty much stress-free when it comes to money?
   YES / NO

4. If you don't feel like cooking on any given night, do you have enough money to go to a restaurant?
   YES / NO

5. If you have been really working hard and want to relax, do you have enough money to comfortably afford a massage or manicure or some other little treat? YES / NO

6. Do you have enough money to comfortably take your kids on vacation?   YES / NO

7. Do you have a vision of how you want your financial future to look?
YES / NO

8. Do you believe you are capable of building a strong financial future?
YES / NO

9. Have you thought of ways you could bring in extra income? YES / NO

10. Do you have good boundaries with your money and avoid spending too much when you can't afford it?
YES / NO

11. If you can't afford it, do you tell your kids no when they ask for something? YES / NO

12. Do you like your job? YES / NO

13. Do you enjoy the work you do? YES / NO

14. Are you treated well at your job? YES / NO

15. Does your job pay you enough to meet your needs? YES / NO

16. Do you get along with your co-workers? YES / NO

17. Do you like your boss? YES / NO

18. Do you have any ideas for a side hustle or second stream of income? YES / NO

19. Do you have decent benefits at your job including health insurance? YES / NO

20. Do you believe that you are capable of building a big, prosperous life for you and your kids, even if aliens take your sugar daddy to Jupiter? YES / NO

Total up your answers here:

YES_____   NO_____

Okay, so here's the thing. Every single person reading this book will, most likely, be in a different position financially and job-wise. So, in an effort to make this more applicable to generally everyone, I am just going to list some things that I think would be helpful across the board. Whether you have no money or you are swimming in the Benjamins, there's always a little room for improvement.

One last thing; I just want to say that, if you are currently in a financial situation that feels hopeless, please know that EVERYTHING can be turned around. Everything can work out. Don't believe me? Let me give you an example.

At one point, in a last-minute effort to avoid foreclosure on my house, I called a consumer credit counseling agency. I explained my situation to the nice lady on the phone and, without skipping a beat she said, "Oh honey, you aren't going to lose your house! You can just file bankruptcy!" I kid you not. After the shock wore off, I felt a sense of horror immediately followed by a sense of freedom. This woman, whom I had never met, was completely confident that my life was going to be 100% okay. And, I don't know what it was but I believed her. Maybe I was desperate for any sliver of hope. I hung up the phone and, even though in the past the thought of bankruptcy would have felt scandalous to me, at this moment, I felt freedom. I felt like I had options. I didn't feel completely doomed.

Anyway, after a short period of feeling hopeful reality began to sink back in. Did I really want to file for bankruptcy? How could I possibly scrape up $17,000 to get my house out of foreclosure when I was living paycheck to paycheck and still not getting my bills paid? I was terrified and filled with anxiety. And I was feeling so completely alone. I was 100% trying to make all of these life-altering decisions all by myself.

But you know what? A few years later and my life is completely different. Using no magic or special tricks, I fought my way out of the financial hole. One day at a time. Literally, one freaking day at a time. And, if I can do it, then you can absolutely do it. Hang in there. Okay, let's get going with some action steps.

<u>Action steps</u>:

1. Get out your notebook or journal. I want you to write down what your dream job is or what the characteristics of your dream job would be. What feelings does your dream job give you? What kind of hours do you work? Do you get to work from home so you can be with your kids more? Do you travel for your job so that you can be away from your kids more? Just kidding! Anyway, just go ahead and write down any and every thing you come up with. And don't forget to be completely honest! If your goal is to find a sugar daddy, write it down. If your goal is never to work again, write it down. If your goal is to win the lottery, write it down. Whatever your true desires are, write them down.

I should mention here that you are by no means required to have grand career plans for yourself. If your goal is to be a stay-at-home mom, I think that's awesome! Or if you have a lifelong dream of volunteering at the food bank, that's genuinely amazing of you! There is absolutely nothing wrong with these goals! We just need to figure out how you are going to have an income in the meantime. So, maybe sit down and envision a job that you can do (and, at least, somewhat enjoy) while working towards your ultimate goal of not working. Or envision how you will approach Grandma to ask for a loan to pay your bills. Whatever works!

2. Now that we have an idea of our dream jobs and our dream incomes, let's start figuring out how we can get there. I want you to make a column for your job category and a column for your finances. In each column I want you to start a list with small, manageable things that you can do every day (or at least a few times a week) to work towards these goals. These things preferably take small amounts of time (I mean we are single moms) and preferably take small amounts of money. Okay, let me give you some examples.

Let's start with your job department first. Let's say you are currently working as a hair stylist but your dream has always been to be a circus clown. You don't hate being a hair stylist and the money is decent, but it's just not what you have always daydreamed of doing for life. So what do you do? Well, since you are currently employed and there are no major issues there, let's start figuring out how you can become a circus clown. Maybe start by spending just ten or fifteen minutes a couple of nights this week googling circus clown schools. Just do a little research on how much it costs, where it's located, how long it is, what the hours are, whether there is financial aid, etc. Then, after a couple of weeks of that, maybe spend a few minutes here and there searching the internet to see if anyone is hiring circus clowns. Maybe look around the web to see what a day in the life of a circus clown looks like. And so on and so on. In other words, just start really small and take lots of little baby steps.

What about if your dream is to be a work-from-home mom? Okay, well, you could maybe dedicate a few minutes a couple of times a week to researching possible work-from-home opportunities. Maybe start thinking about products or services that feel good to you and see if there is a way you could sell them. Maybe set up an Etsy shop? Maybe take an online class to learn coding or billing or something else you can do at home? There are probably a million ideas out there but, as with everything else, you have to start with some good old research and Google searching. And that costs nothing! Also, did you know that there are lots of single mom groups on Facebook? I mention this here because I am in several and there are always posts going around about work-from-home job ideas and opportunities. Maybe something to check out.

And what about if you absolutely hate your current job? Well, that's not okay. The stress is so darn bad for you. Several years ago, when I was working at a job that I absolutely hated, I felt stuck and hopeless. I didn't even have the energy to read the want ads when I got home from work. I stayed at the job because it had a flexible schedule and I could be with my kids more. But if you are questioning whether or not stress is bad for you, let me just go ahead and reassure you that it is VERY bad for you. While I was at this job, my anger levels were sky high, I gained thirty pounds, and I was exhausted nonstop. My hair literally started falling out. And I would come home from work and start snapping at my kids. Yikes. Oh yeah, other stressful things were going on in my life at the same time, but that job was at the top of the list.

Anyway, it's really not okay to stay stuck forever at a job you hate. So, what can you do today to start getting the heck out of there? Well, as hard as it may seem, try to find the energy to start looking around. Maybe try setting up a new resume on Indeed. If you set up a resume and fill out the info on Indeed and then make it "public", people will start coming to you! And it's 100% free.

Anyway, my point here is that there are always plenty of little ways (that are usually free!) to start moving in the direction you want to go. And, oftentimes, when you start making these small movements, the universe will see that you are ready for something new. Something different. And it will start helping you out.

Okay, now let me give you an example for your finances column. Do you want to be financially free? Depending on your current situation, there is always something you can do to work towards a better future. Are you in financial ruin and barely able to hang on? Okay, I have been there and done that and I 100% feel your pain. This situation can feel so terribly hopeless. So, what's one small thing you can do this week? Well, maybe start by sitting down and writing down every single thing you owe. Acknowledging where you stand is super helpful. Or, honestly, maybe just commit to yourself saying that you will not take out another payday loan this week, no matter what. Or maybe you'll pay ONE extra dollar on your credit card bill. Believe me, I have been to the bottom of financial hell and I know exactly how much of a nightmare it is. But I also know that you can dig your way out even when it seems completely impossible. As tremendously scary as it is, calling your creditors and trying to work something out is usually helpful. And it might make you feel better that you took some action. Another great idea would be to commit to going to the library this week and checking out one finance/money-related book. That will let the universe know that you mean business.

This may seem a little out there but, seriously, when you are completely broke, you are usually willing to try anything. Or, at least, I was. Anyway, I would suggest doing some Google searches on the Law of Attraction. I know it might not be your cup of tea and that's totally okay. But it doesn't cost anything to check out Pinterest and maybe you will actually love the info you find! But, in short, the Law of Attraction is a principle based on the idea that you attract into your life people, things, and situations that are like you and match how you feel and what you believe. So, if you FEEL rich, you will attract more wealth. If you FEEL broke, you will attract more debt. Or something along those lines. Anyway, I think it's something interesting to check out and could be helpful to learn about.

And, lastly, if you are doing okay financially, then maybe commit to saving a little more or start reading up on investing. Maybe dedicate forty-five minutes this week to putting together a sophisticated budget and start prioritizing what you want to spend money on. If nothing else, a great idea would be to commit to checking out from the library and reading at least one book a month that is financial/money-management related. There are a million great books on money and knowledge is always power! And look, when you do become super-rich and have trillions of dollars, you are going to want to know how to invest it properly, right? So why not start getting ready now?

3. Now that we have grasped what we want our careers/jobs/sources of income and our finances to look like and we have started taking some little actions towards them, let's start feeling them. How do we do that? Well, start by getting out the fine China that you inherited from Aunt Sue. And that bologna sandwich you are having for lunch? Yep, eat it on the expensive plate. Doing some shopping and walk past the high-end jewelry store? Go in! Go in and browse around and soak in the feeling of all the pretty jewels. Going to the grocery? Put on your diamond earrings!

As cooky as it sounds, doing all of these things will help you FEEL rich and abundant and worthy. And this can help you start attracting more riches and abundance and worthiness. And that sounds darn good to me!

You may have heard this a million times before but start making it a practice to acknowledge all of the things you are grateful for, even when it feels like not much. Are your kids healthy? Did your car start today? Did you make it through the entire day without crying? Did you find five dollars in the sofa? Did someone tell you you looked pretty today?

When you start adding up all the things you are grateful for, you will begin to (maybe slowly at first) feel more abundant. And when you start feeling more abundant, life feels better and better things start coming your way.

Being a single mom usually means that we are on our own when it comes to bringing home the bacon. And I would bet my little bit of money that none of us daydream about spending the rest of our lives hustling and working ourselves to death to live paycheck to paycheck. So, until we win the lottery or Prince Charming the billionaire comes along, we should probably put some effort into building a source of income that makes us happy. And in the meantime, go ahead and wear your best jewelry to the dollar store.

Chapter 7:
The Three of Us

Have you and your kids ever been to the Grand Canyon? No? We haven't either. But….it's on my list of things I really want to do with my kids. I also really want to take them to the Cheyenne Frontier Days in Wyoming. And I want to take them camping in Canada. And while I'm at it, I really want to take them to Europe.

Do you have a running list of things you want to do/see/experience with your kids? Just you and them? Maybe it has nothing to do with travel. Maybe you dream about starting a Sunday night ritual of having a sit-down family dinner of steak and potatoes. Or maybe you dream about doing a beach photo shoot of you and your babies dressed in matching outfits. Or maybe you have always wanted to start a family project like a vegetable garden.

Regardless of what they are, I would imagine that, somewhere in your mind, there are hopes and dreams you have for just you and your kids. Maybe some trip you want to take or tradition you want to start or a project you want to do together; something that involves just you and your kids experiencing life and making good old memories.

Well, you guessed it; we are going to start working on putting these dreams into action. No matter how big or small our dreams are there is always something we can do today to start working towards them. So let's get going.

Okay, so since we already know that we have hopes and dreams for ourselves and our kids, no need for a quiz here. Instead, we are cutting straight to the chase. In place of a quiz, I will list some categories that you can read through and think about to discover where your biggest dreams may be. And then we will head to our action steps. Let's get started.

Get out your notebook and pen. Read through the following categories and make some notes about any ideas that come to mind. Don't hold back. Write down any and all ideas that come up. Big and small. Just put it all down on paper for now.

Things I want us to do:

1. Do you have vacations that you dream of taking your kids on?

2. Are there places in your current city that you would like to take your kids? Maybe local sights like museums, monuments, memorials, theaters, etc.

3. Are there restaurants you really want to take your kids to?

4. Are there foods you want to try with your kids?

5. Are there foods you want to teach your kids to cook?

6. Are there people you want to take your kids to visit? Family members,

friends? Or maybe you have loved ones that have passed away and you would like to visit the cemetery with your kids and tell them about the person.

7. Are there traditions you want to start with your kids?

8. Do you want to make a scrapbook or a memory box with your kids?

9. Do you want to take a class together with your kids or learn a foreign language together?

10. Do you want to plant a tree or garden together?

11. Do you want to build something together or do some sort of project together?

12. Do you want to make Halloween costumes together?

13. Do you want to start a tradition of making candy apples for the first cold day of fall?

14. Do you want to commit to having dinner at the dinner table at least three nights a week?

15. Do you want to set aside one day a month where you do something fun like going to the movies and out to dinner or going to the zoo?

16. Do you want to make a change jar where you save together for a special activity?

17. Do you want to volunteer at a soup kitchen together once a month?

18. Do you want to have board game nights on Friday nights?

19. Do you want to have a photo shoot done together?

20. Do you want to take a road trip to the Grand Canyon?

21. Do you want to buy a tent and take your kids camping?

22. Do you want to take surf lessons together in Bali?

I could seriously go on and on forever! There are so many possible ways you can spend time together and make incredible memories with your kids. And they can cost zero money or they can cost oodles of money. But what's most important is that you are spending good old quality time with your kids and living your best lives.

Okay. So let's get to work on living these dreams! Here are your action steps.

Action steps:

1. Make a list of all of the things you want to do. Now, I want you to separate these things into three categories. Category number one is things that cost relatively little or no money. So you will need no time to save up for them. For instance, having dinner together three nights a week. Category number two is things that don't cost a tremendous amount of money and you can afford to do them once or twice a month; for instance, going to a movie and dinner or buying the materials for a scrapbook. Category number three is the higher-dollar items that may require some saving for a few months (maybe even a year). This might include a vacation, a photo shoot session, or the materials to build a garden.

2. Now that you have the three categories, I want you to go through each one and list the items in the order in which you want to do them. For instance, are you dying to do the photo shoot but the garden can wait until

next summer? Or are you desperate to take that vacation and not as desperate to go to the zoo and amusement park again? Go through each category and put them in order from most wanted now to "I want to do it, but it can wait."

3. Now you have three groups of things that you can get started on today! Let's say the top items on your three lists are: have Friday night board game night, build a bookcase together, and take a trip to Tahiti together. Well, you can start working on all three today. Decide that next Friday night is your inaugural board game night. Start researching plans and costs for your bookcase. And, empty out a jar to start your savings for Tahiti! Woo-hoo!

Okay, how did that go? Feeling excited about making some seriously awesome memories with your favorite people? Great!

If you want to keep this train moving, here are some bonus points you can do.

Bonus Points!

1. Get your kids involved! Instead of having Friday night be game night, how about make it a night of brainstorming. You can get some popcorn and some notebooks and, together, come up with any and all, big and small, ideas for things you can do together. Your kids may have some ideas that you would have never even thought of but that would be meaningful to them.

    For a few years after getting divorced, I didn't send out Christmas cards. Before getting divorced, every year I took a bunch of Christmasy pictures of my kids and picked my favorite for the annual holiday card. Well, after my divorce, one year my daughter asked me if we were going to do a Christmas card that year. And it occurred to me that just maybe that had been something that was important to her. Maybe she loved that tradition. And I instantly felt sad that I had not continued doing it. I liked doing it but, honestly, it was not the biggest deal to me. But maybe to her, it was.

So why not get the kids in on making future plans!

2. While you are in the mode of getting the kids involved, why not get them to help out with saving for it. Have them help you make coin jars where you all pitch in coins to save for that movie night. Sounds to me like a bonus lesson on finances!

   Okay, I have to be honest with you here. Being this organized and creative was really NOT me on most days. Most days I was just hoping to get my hair brushed. But if you can manage to accomplish things like this, you are rocking it sister. And I really do believe that the memories made will be some of your children's greatest treasures.

Doing amazing things and having great experiences with your kids is 100% possible.

And it can cost as little or as much as you want it to. Most importantly, you will be seriously making some incredible memories that your kids will treasure some day. And how good does that feel?!

Chapter 8:
Wishing and hoping

Do you have a bucket list? Just for you? No kids included here? Only you?

Do you have any secret goals or secret wishes that have always stayed in the back of your mind? Is there something you always wanted to do but, for whatever reason, just haven't? Is there something you always wanted to learn? Somewhere you always wanted to go?

I'll go first. I have always wanted to be a spinning class instructor. Yep, seriously. I have daydreamed about wearing the cute little workout clothes with my cute little toned body and getting everyone hyped up with my amazing soundtrack. I would be sweaty and happy and the cool girl on the block. But…that's all a daydream. The reality, at the moment, is that I don't have the cute little exercise outfit, I don't have the cute little toned body, and I am not getting anyone hyped up. Especially not my two teenagers. Oof.

And cows. Yep. I daydream about living on a beautiful farm with cows out grazing in the pasture. I wake up and drink my coffee in the crisp morning air, on my back porch, while I look out over the green grass fields at my cows. Life is slow and peaceful and happy. And all the grandkids come over on the weekends to play in the fields, see the cows, and help me bake apple pies. Aaahhhh.

Maybe you always wanted to learn to speak French and then go to Paris, eat croissants, drink red wine, and visit the Eiffel Tower. All while wearing your beret.

Or maybe you always envisioned yourself soaking up the rays on a sunny California beach after you spent the morning learning to surf.

Or maybe you always wanted to go to cooking school and learn how to make little tarts and pastries and other yummy things.

Or maybe you always knew that one day you would start that non-profit to help abused women or single moms who could use some help.

I know that somewhere in the back of your mind are some hopes and dreams, maybe some that you have had since childhood; maybe some brand-new ones. What are they?

I know that we are single moms. I know that life hasn't necessarily gone exactly as we may have hoped. I know that we are often exhausted, financially-strapped, short on time, and overwhelmed by our daily lives and responsibilities. I know that our children come before us. I really do. I get all of it. But I still believe that we can hold on to our hopes and dreams, no matter how "crazy," or out there, or far-fetched they may seem.

And here's the thing. We may not live to see every single one of our dreams come true. Who knows? But we also very well may live to see several of them come true! And how amazing and exciting is that?

So, this chapter is about YOU. This chapter is about declaring your dreams to the universe and shouting out to the powers that be that these are your dreams and you understand that some may not work out but, gosh darn it, some of them just might.

I will say it here again. Think about your kids. Would you ever tell them to quit dreaming, wishing, and hoping? If your daughter were to become a single mom, would you tell her to go ahead and hang up her hat and give up on the rest of her life? Would you ever tell her to go ahead and give up on ever finding love again? If your son went through a rough financial patch, would you ever advise him to just give up on all of his goals and hopes of owning a beautiful home someday? If your daughter were to gain twenty extra pounds in college, would you ever tell her to throw in the towel on her dream of one day being a marathon runner? No? Never? Okay. Well then, why on Earth would you EVER give up on any of your hopes and dreams? I mean, yea, if you are eighty-five years old and a great-grandmother, you could maybe go ahead and realize that your dream of becoming a Dallas Cowboys cheerleader is probably becoming less likely to happen. But you never know!

Anyway, whether our hopes and dreams are "realistic" or not, we are going to honor them today. So, let's get started.

The quiz I have for you here is to help you get the juices flowing in your dreams department. Remember, lots of "no" answers is just a little sign that this area could use some improvement. Here we go:

<u>Dreams Quiz</u>:

1. Do you have hopes and dreams for yourself that you often daydream about? YES / NO

2. Do you think it's okay to have hopes and dreams for yourself? YES / NO

3. Do you ever give yourself time to think about, plan, or work on the hopes and dreams you have for yourself? YES / NO

4. Have you ever written down your goals and hopes and dreams for yourself? YES / NO

5. Do you believe you have a bright future ahead for yourself? YES / NO

6. Do you believe that you are worthy of having your own hopes and dreams? YES / NO

7. Do you believe that you deserve to have good things for yourself? YES / NO

8. Do you believe that you are capable of doing what you set your mind to? YES / NO

9. Are you able to see beyond your life as a single mom? YES / NO

10. Do you feel hopeful and not negative when you think of the future? YES / NO

11. If I asked you right now to tell me one dream you have for yourself, would you even be able to come up with one? YES / NO

Total up your answers here:

YES_____   NO_____

Okay. So those are just a few things to think about.

Before we move on to our action steps, I want you to consider something else. I know that it's very possible that you are a single mom of young children. I know that you may be swamped with responsibility and overwhelmed with your life right now. I know that you may just be trying to survive sleepless nights and diaper changes and working a nine-to-five job. I know that you may have less money in your bank account than the cost of a pizza. I know that you may be thinking that I am certifiably crazy for even suggesting that you think about yourself and your hopes and dreams. I get it. I really do. But I want you to do this so that you don't lose sight of you. I want you to remember that you are important too. I want you to have something to hope for when you are bent over crying because your child is away at Dad's for the first time. I want you to have something to pray for when you are overcome with loneliness. I want you to have something to work on and get excited about when you feel convinced that your ex is doing better than you. I want you to have so much hope for your future.

And....I want you to remember that, as impossible and as scary as it seems, one day your kids will grow up. One day they will leave home. One day they will move on to their own adult lives. And, as heartbreaking (and, okay, maybe exciting sometimes) as that sounds, it's the truth. And if you are anything like me you just might want to have something else to think about and focus on so that you aren't completely overcome with wishing they would come back. Phew.

So, here's to us and building our hopes and dreams! Let's get started.

<u>Action Steps</u>:

1. Okay, so break out your trusty old notebook or piece of paper again. And you guessed it; we are going to make another list. I want you to list every single hope or dream or wish that you have ever had for just yourself. Big and small.

   For example, I might write down things like:

   I want a farm with cows and a swimming pool and a pretty view.
   I want to get married again someday.
   I want one of the new Ford Broncos that are coming out.
   I want to go to Canada.
   I want to get my body into super healthy shape.
   I want to be the happiest I have ever been at the age of fifty.
   I want to make a career out of writing books that I think might help others.
   I want to learn to speak Italian.

As usual, I could go on forever and ever.

Anyway, I want you to write down all of your hopes that are just for you.

2. Alright, I want you to make a vision board. Never heard of a vision board? No worries. A vision board is just a place (usually a cork board or bulletin board or something like that) where you place images and words that represent your desires. You can cut and paste anything that represents your hopes and dreams onto the board. And then, as often as you can, look at the board! If you want a little more direction, just Google vision boards and I am sure there will be plenty of info.

A little woo-woo? Maybe. But I really believe they work! And it doesn't matter how crazy big your dreams are or how far in the future they might be. Put them on the darn board! Just go through your list and find images or words or whatever that fits your goal. And note that your vision board can change over time. I am continually updating my vision board and removing things when they don't feel right anymore. Remember, focus on the feeling of what you want when picking things for your board.

Here are some examples:

Want to go to Africa? If it were me, I would search "Africa" on Pinterest or Google and find images of Africa that feel good and feel right to me. Just trust your gut and go with it. Everyone will have different feelings. Then, when you have found images that feel right to you, just print them out and stick them on the board. Voila! Don't have a printer? No worries. Try to get your hands on some magazines that vibe with what you are dreaming about. Like before, want to go to Africa? Okay, great. Head to the store and look for some travel magazines. Or steal them from the doctor's office. Just kidding. An even better idea might be to search the internet for travel companies that offer trips to Africa. Fill out the request form on their website and ask them to send you some brochures. Completely free!

3. Okay, now is the most important part! Put your vision board where you can look at it AT LEAST once a day. And you guessed it; look at it!! Give yourself a solid couple of minutes to stare at it. Really stare. And as you look at each picture, FEEL what it would feel like to be living that dream right now. Again, want to go to Africa? When you look at your image of Africa on your board, feel what you think it would feel like to actually be in Africa. What would you be wearing? It would probably be warm and you might be sweating a little, right? What would it smell like? What sounds would you hear? Maybe lions roaring or the ocean waves. What would you be doing? Going on a safari, maybe, or visiting a friend in the city? Who would you be with? And so on and so on. Just get into it. You can also take a picture of your vision board and use it as a screensaver for your phone and there are also vision board apps.

And before we leave the subject of vision boards, I should mention that this can be used in all areas of your life. Not just your wildest dreams. Hope that date you got asked on goes well? Put a picture of a happy couple on your vision board and envision the date going perfectly. It might not always happen, but hey, it could!

Okay. How did that go? At the very least, I hope that this exercise has given you permission to start remembering your dreams. I hope this has allowed you a few minutes to indulge in the idea that your life is, by no means, anywhere near over. You are just getting started! There is so much ahead and so many things to get excited about in the future. And you deserve every single one of them.

Alrighty, here we go. Our last round of bonus points. Why not go out with a bang and do them all!

<u>Bonus Points</u>!

1. Feeling like you can do a little more work on your hopes and dreams? Excellent! Let's do like before and separate our dreams into small, medium, and giant-sized. Make three lists and, just like we did before, we will put them in order of how important they are to us. Next, start with number one on each list and figure out how you can take some baby steps towards that dream. Want to learn French? Go check out a French-language instructional CD from the library and listen to it on your way to work. Want to go to Argentina? After your kids go to bed tonight, spend five minutes searching the internet for travel companies that offer trips to Argentina and request some free brochures. Yes, you guessed it! You can then add the pictures of Argentina to your vision board. Want to find your future husband? Go buy the perfect date outfit so that you will have it ready to go in case you meet him tomorrow!

2. Dive deeper into working on your vision board and your manifesting. Maybe commit more time to gazing at your vision board every day. Or start meditating on your dreams. Or commit to visualizing your goals every night as you drift off to sleep.

   A great idea would be to head to the library and check out some books or audiobooks on the power of visualization, manifestation, and setting intentions. Even if that seems a little woo-woo for you, you won't know until you try it! Yeah, some of it is a bit out there, but the basic idea seems legit to me. At the end of this book, I include a list of books and movies and other resources that I have found to be really helpful over the years. Maybe you will find something there that you like.

3. Make it a point to take some risks. No, I don't mean you should sell your car and buy a plane ticket to Argentina. I mean step out of your comfort zone. Do more things that you have been scared to do in the past. For instance, want to learn French? Sign up for a

French class instead of listening to tapes in your car. Want to find your future husband? Sign up for that French class! He just might be sitting at the desk next to yours!

A couple of years ago, I was starting to get sick and tired of being me. I was tired of being a hermit. I was tired of hiding from the world because I was ashamed of myself. I was tired of feeling lonely because I never socialized anymore.

But, I was also scared. I was scared of saying yes to a friend invite and then regretting it when I got there and had a horrible time. Or what if I was brave and ventured out to a restaurant and my ex-husband and his new wife and baby were there? Or what if I put aside my embarrassment about my body and went to a party and the man of my dreams was there and I was mortified?

Eventually, I made a choice to just risk it and start putting myself back out there. And you know what? I had the best time! I actually had real honest fun! For the first time in YEARS. And not a single one of my fears came true.

I am saying all of this because, if you have found yourself hiding from the world and getting really tired of it, I urge you to go ahead and get out there! I can't guarantee that none of your fears will come true. But I do know that, if you keep waiting for the perfect time to do it, it will never come.

One amazing aspect of putting myself out there and starting to live again was that, when I did it, more and more good things started happening. My life started improving. New friends showed up. More money came. More happiness came. I found myself feeling happy and excited for literally no reason. I believe that, when I gathered the courage to get back into life, the universe started rewarding me.

I hope these tips get you on your way to giving life to your hopes and dreams. I hope you feel a little more wishful and a little more hopeful. Most importantly, I hope you feel a little more convinced that you are worthy of the most amazing life.

Here's what I know. Although it may seem like it, I didn't write this book for you. I mean, yes, of course I wrote it for you, but I also wrote it for me. I wrote it to give myself the nudge to build my best life. I wrote it to remind myself of every single thing I have written in this book. I wrote it because, honestly, a LOT of the time I make bad choices. A LOT of the time I stick to routine and what's comfortable. A LOT of the time I am scared of change. A LOT of the time I am just too damn tired to look at my freaking vision board. Well, to be completely honest, sometimes I want to throw the vision board out the window and run it over with my car. And, seriously, sometimes I need my own darn pep talk.

Here's something else I know. It's okay if you put down this book and eat a bag of potato chips and watch Netflix for the next seven hours. It's okay if you read my words about meditating and want to punch me in the face. It's okay if you straight up laugh out loud when I say it's okay to dream about going to Argentina and you are three months behind on your freaking mortgage. I seriously understand.

Several years ago, when I was barely hanging on, I may have wanted to punch you too if you suggested to me that I dream about spending a week surfing in California. Or, more likely, I would have cried. Ugh.

What I am trying to say here is that I have been there. I have been broke, lonely, desperate, scared to death, angry beyond belief, jealous, majorly depressed, anxious, unhealthy, overweight, defeated, hopeless, filled with despair, mad at the world, and on and on and on. I have, at one time or another, been ALL of the things. There were LOTS of times when I couldn't see a future for myself that wasn't all of the above. There were lots of times when I was sure I would never be happy again. There were many times when I was sure I would be lonely, broke, and exhausted forever.

I still have a ways to go. I still haven't been to Canada! And I still haven't met my future husband! But…. I have come an incredibly long way from those days of exhaustion, despair, and hopelessness. I can say, without a doubt, that I am happy now.

More than anything, I want you to be happy. Being a single mom is so freaking hard and, as far as I know, no awards or prizes are being given out for doing a good job. So, I am here today to pat you on the back. YOU are doing a fantastic job! I'm serious; I just know that you are crushing it. Even on the days when you cry yourself to sleep. Even on the days when all you feed your kids is gummy bears because you are just too exhausted to come up with anything else. Even on the days when you wish your kids' stepmom would be taken away on a spaceship to Mars. Even on the days when you can't control yourself and you hit send on that nasty text to your ex. Even on the days when you say, "Screw it," and go get your nails done instead of paying that past due bill. I know. It happens.

Even with all of those days combined, you are still doing an absolutely amazing job! You are doing the very best that you can and that is what counts. You love your kids more than anything and that is what matters. You are trying to be the best single momma and that's what it's all about.

When I look back on my days as a single mom, sure, I will see the utter exhaustion, and the days filled with despair, and the times I was so angry I felt like my eyeballs might pop out. But I will also see how it has shaped me into the person I am now. I am stronger. I am more compassionate for those who are struggling. I am humbler. And I see what a blessing it can be to go through tough times. And I wouldn't trade a single second of it.

I hope this book has given you some doable ideas for building a life you love. I really hope that you can look back one day and see how crazy beautiful your time as a single mom has been. I hope you realize how beautiful, strong, and amazing you are. And, most importantly, I hope that you never, ever forget that, in the eyes of your kids, you, my dear, are a HERO.

<u>Things I Love</u>:

    I decided I would make a list of things that really helped me along the way. I don't know, some (or all?) of this stuff may not resonate with you, but I figured it can't hurt to list it in case it's really beneficial to someone. And the best part is everything I am listing here should be free to you in some way or form. Whether it's a YouTube video or a book you can check out at the library or a movie that's on Netflix; whatever it is, I am hoping that there is little or no cost involved if you want to check it out. I hope this is helpful!

    No, I am not getting paid or anything (I wish!) to list these. I just really found value in them. And, to be honest, I don't necessarily agree with every single word in every one of these resources; but, overall, I really love the vibe of these. Oh, and these are in no way in any particular order. I like them each so much in their own way and really could never rank them.

    I hope you enjoy!

<u>Books</u>:

1. *You are a Badass,* by Jen Sincero

2. *You are a Badass at Making Money,* by Jen Sincero

3. *Girl, Wash Your Face,* by Rachel Hollis

4. *This Messy Magnificent Life,* by Geneen Roth

5. *May Cause Miracles,* by Gabrielle Bernstein

6. *Untamed,* by Glennon Doyle

7. *He's Just Not That Into You,* by Greg Behrendt and Liz Tuccillo

8. *Think and Grow Rich,* by Napoleon Hill

9. *You Can Heal Your Life,* by Louise Hay

10. *The Secret,* by Rhonda Byrne

11. *The Subtle Art of Not Giving a F*ck,* by Mark Manon

12. *The Universe Has Your Back,* by Gabrielle Bernstein

13. *The Power of Intention,* by Wayne Dyer

14. *Get Out of Your Own Way,* by Dave Hollis

15. *Becoming Mrs. Stanley: The Single Mom's Guide to Attracting Mr. Right!,* by Karen Stanley

16. *Hungry for Happiness,* by Samantha Skelly

17. *Your Second Life Begins When You Realize You Only Have One,* by Raphaelle Giordano

Movies/videos:

1. *The Pursuit of Happyness*

2. *The Shift* – this is a film by Wayne Dyer

3. *I am Not Your Guru* – this is the Tony Robbins documentary on Netflix

4. *The Secret*

5. *Your Value* – YouTube video by Ben Lionel Scott, my all-time favorite!

Podcasts:

1. *The Rise Podcast with Rachel Hollis*

2. *The Tony Robbins Podcast*

3. *The Papaya Podcast*

4. *The Wayne Dyer Podcast*

5. *The Wellness Mama Podcast*

6. *The Balanced Blonde*

7. *The School of Greatness Podcast*

8. *The Manifestation Babe Podcast*

9. *The Inner Integration Podcast*

10. *You Can Heal Your Life Podcast*

11. The Unstuck Podcast with Shawn Mynar

12. *The Hungry For Happiness Podcast*

Thank you so much for reading!

I hope you have enjoyed reading this as much as I have enjoyed writing it.

It would mean so much to me if you would leave a review for my book! You can return to Amazon or wherever you made the purchase and should be able to easily leave a review. Thank you so much!

You can always keep in touch with me by following me on Facebook and Instagram @summerlinconner

Be sure to join my Facebook group for single mommas! Just look for *Single Moms Building Big Lives* Facebook group. See you there!

You can also find more info and sign up for my newsletter at www.summerlinconner.com

And, lastly, you can always email me at

summerlin@summerlinconner.com

I would love to hear from you!

NOTES:

NOTES:

NOTES:

NOTES:

NOTES:

NOTES:

NOTES:

NOTES:

Summerlin Conner is an author, Registered Nurse, and mom of two great kids. Summerlin's first book is *The Three of Us: A Brutally Honest, Often Hilarious, and Sometimes Heartbreaking Memoir of One Mom's Adventures in Single Parenting*. Summerlin and her kids live outside of New Orleans, Louisiana.

CPSIA information can be obtained
at www.ICGtesting.com
Printed in the USA
LVHW111708141220
674152LV00028B/446

9 781734 559132